P9-AFI-084

WILLIAM SAROYAN

A Study of the Short Fiction

Also available in Twayne's Studies in Short Fiction Series

Twayne's Studies in Short Fiction

Gordon Weaver, General Editor
Oklahoma State University

WILLIAM SAROYAN
(1913–1981)
Portrait by Alice Notley

WILLIAM SAROYAN

A Study of the Short Fiction

Edward Halsey Foster
Stevens Institute of Technology

TWAYNE PUBLISHERS • NEW YORK
Maxwell Macmillan Canada • Toronto
Maxwell Macmillan International • New York Oxford Singapore Sydney

Twayne's Studies in Short Fiction Series, No. 26

Copyright © 1991 by Twayne Publishers

Twayne Publishers
Macmillan Publishing Company
866 Third Avenue
New York, NY 10022

Maxwell Macmillan Canada, Inc.
1200 Eglinton Avenue East
Suite 200
Don Mills, Ontario M3C 3N1

Macmillan Publishing Company is part of the Maxwell Communication Group of Companies.

Library of Congress Cataloging-in-Publication Data

Foster, Edward Halsey.
   William Saroyan : a study of the short fiction / Edward Halsey Foster.
     p.   cm. — (Twayne's studies in short fiction ; no. 26)
   Includes bibliographical references and index.
   ISBN 0-8057-8335-0
   1. Saroyan, William, 1908–1981—Criticism and interpretation.
2. Short story. I. Title. II. Series.
   PS3537.A826Z67   1991
   813'.52—dc20
                                             91-22003
                                               CIP

Copyediting supervised by Barbara Sutton.
Book production and design by Janet Z. Reynolds.
Typeset by Compset, Inc., Beverly, Massachusetts.

10 9 8 7 6 5 4 3 2 1

For Edith D. Foster,
Betty Derosia,
and Roy C. Foster

Have you thought there could be but a single supreme?
There can be any number of supremes—one does not
   countervail another any more than one eyesight
   countervails another or one life countervails
   another.
All is eligible to all,
All is for individuals, all is for you,
No condition is prohibited, not God's or any.

> —Walt Whitman, "By Blue Ontario's Shore"

Contents

Contents

Preface

Much of William Saroyan's short fiction is first-person narrative, and the speaker is usually Saroyan himself. It doesn't matter whether the story comes out of something he actually did or saw (although in fact much of the fiction is autobiographical); what matters is a characteristic set of attitudes, a certain personality or presence for which the narrative is merely an agent. Even when the "I" is not used, it is commonly Saroyan who is talking about his opinions, his family, or something in his past. The stories, one might say, are spoken, not written.

Saroyan's fiction could hardly be further from the aesthetics of point of view, which Percy Lubbock codified in *The Craft of Fiction* (1921). Simplifying ideas he had found in his master, Henry James, Lubbock argued that a "narrative . . . must represent the story-teller's ordered and arranged experience, and . . . must accordingly be of the nature of a picture." He felt this narrative should be "raise[d] to a power approaching that of drama, where the intervention of story-teller is no longer felt."[1] But in Saroyan, what matters most is the fact of the story-teller's presence. Saroyan does not present a well-ordered "picture" giving an illusion of objectivity, as if the writer and his fiction were distinct, but rather uses narrative as the expression of a subjective identity. In Saroyan's mind that identity is in turn not merely personal or solipsistic, for it is in its essential nature "ethnic"; it is the expression of the group and the heritage to which the writer owes his identity.[2]

Behind that assumption is a long aesthetic history in America that can be traced back at least as far as Whitman, who believed his poems spoke as much for Americans generally as for himself. Whitman was an important writer for Saroyan, but the more immediate influences were James Joyce, Gertrude Stein, and particularly Sherwood Anderson. They, rather than the nineteenth-century writers admired by Lubbock, were his models, and Saroyan became in effect a second-generation modernist, seeking in fiction, as Joyce did, "the uncreated conscience of [his] race."[3] Stein's subjective use of language in *Tender Buttons* may have influenced him, too, but the greatest influence, as he repeatedly acknowledged, was Anderson.

In the early 1920s Anderson was one of America's most influential writers, but by the time Saroyan began to publish, critical fashions were moving toward a renascent realism exemplified by "proletarian fiction." Anderson was attacked in the critical journals, and so was Saroyan. Most of Saroyan's books sold well, and most book reviewers liked him, but critics on the Left (and they were the most interesting critics around) were generally hostile when they did not ignore him altogether. The very nature of Saroyan's politics (or *apparent* lack of politics) made him unacceptable. He was ideologically incorrect.

Subsequent critical schools were, in general, equally incapable of understanding what Saroyan was doing, and he was accused during the 1940s and 1950s, for example, of not giving enough attention to "technique" and "form." Lubbock's shade had returned, and Saroyan, together with Anderson, had always been one of his chief opponents. New Critics in particular, insisting that fiction must be well crafted, failed to realize that craft is, after all, convention, and had Saroyan followed their standards his prose would have lost the spontaneity and improvisation characteristic of his best-known works. As the New Criticism solidified its influence in the universities, his stories began to disappear from even the few classroom anthologies to which he had, however surreptitiously, been admitted. Toward the end of the 1950s, according to Lawrence Lipton, his "early stories [were being] sought out in yellowing paperbacks" by beat writers,[4] but that kind of attention would never impress the universities, where the beats themselves were an anathema.

One thing that attracted beat writers to Saroyan was the immediacy they found in his stories. Those stories were quick, sharp exercises, improvised like jazz. Saroyan, who claimed that between 1934 and 1939 he had written 500 stories, was certainly one of the most prolific writers of his generation. Many of his stories were written in a single day, some in a few hours. Most of the stories in his first book, *The Daring Young Man on the Flying Trapeze* (1934), were written in the same month, one story every day—apparently just to see whether he could do it.

Saroyan, as his followers knew, was one of the few writers who could try something like that and get away with it. The stories (at least the best of them) preserved the rhythms of spoken English, together with a freshness and grace they might well have lost had he taken greater care and conscientiously followed Lubbock's rules. Saroyan simply wrote, and wrote fast, not letting preconceptions about what a story should or should not do take control. For him it worked—or at least it worked often enough to convince him that he was doing things the right way.

Much that he published went directly from the typewriter to the typesetter. Weldon Kees, reviewing *Love, Here Is My Hat* in 1938, attacked "Saroyan's flair for being able to grind [his works] out in wholesale lots, and letting the stories fall where they may."[5] *Love, Here Is My Hat* is one of Saroyan's less successful books, but what Kees says could apply to any of the collections. All of them contain stories one suspects Saroyan rarely or never reread—in any case, surely never revised in a major way. On the other hand, in every book there are excellent stories that may in a sense have been as hastily or thoughtlessly written as those which do not succeed. What matters in his stories is above all the sound and personality of the narrator, and it is clear that for Saroyan to get those qualities onto the page, paying careful attention to the "rules" and the construction of his work was much less effective than simply writing one story after another until finally, magically, he wrote one in which everything came together.

And in fact that happened often. The best of Saroyan's stories are found in *The Daring Young Man on the Flying Trapeze*, *Inhale and Exhale*, and *My Name Is Aram*. To these should be added a few works from the late 1930s, the title story from *The Assyrian and Other Stories*, and some of his last works collected in *Madness in the Family*. Altogether there are four or five volumes of remarkable work.

Any attempt to come to terms with Saroyan's stories should start with the aesthetic assumptions that lie behind them. Although little would be gained by measuring the stories against standards he intentionally rejected, it is helpful to examine criticisms that were directed at them. One often senses a struggle between diametric positions on what literature, and indeed language, can or should accomplish—a struggle, that is, between critics who want literature to express a particular ideology or to follow certain conventions of literary form (two positions that can be versions of the same thing) and writers like Saroyan who understand language basically as an instrument of personal expression. But Saroyan's aesthetics also imply more of a political position than he generally admitted, at least directly. In other words, the problem, as we will see, was not simply that Saroyan refused to go along with his critics but that his kind of writing implied a political ideal, anarchistic and libertarian, that threatened their own.

Whatever problems Saroyan posed for academic critics, he clearly extended an American literary tradition that was rooted in Whitman and that would have the greatest consequence for the next generation of writers. To many young writers in the 1950s Saroyan was absolutely "canonical," and their judgment still appears valid. When his sense of ethnic identity, his aesthetics, and his craftsmanship coalesce, the result is a story of a very high order. Perhaps one sign of good writing (provided, of course, that the writing is serious and not merely put together for the market) is that it simply refuses to go away, no matter how hostile its critics may be. And Saroyan does not go away.

In Part 1 of this volume I discuss first the major stories in *The Daring Young Man on the Flying Trapeze* (1934) and their specifically Armenian sensibility. I examine the expressionist aesthetics developed by Sherwood Anderson and adopted by Saroyan at the beginning of his career and show its importance to the major stories in *Inhale and Exhale* and *Three Times Three*, both published in 1936. I also discuss the leftist critical attitudes of the time and the general hostility toward Saroyan by Marxist and, later, formalist critics. The stories written in the late 1930s, which reflect Saroyan's work as a scriptwriter, are, after the promise of his early work, generally disappointing, but *My Name Is Aram* (1940) is a major achievement, Saroyan's most unified collection of short fiction. *The Human Comedy*, although generally considered a novel, is viewed as a series of interrelated short stories like *My Name Is Aram*. I also explore the various reasons for the decline in the number and quality of stories in the late 1940s and 1950s, when Saroyan began writing memoirs. And I conclude Part 1 with an examination of Saroyan's posthumously published collection of short fiction, *Madness in the Family* and with a brief discussion of his influence on later expressionist writers, particularly Jack Kerouac.

I am deeply grateful to James H. Maguire and Leo Hamalian for their encouragement during my work on Saroyan, to Ted Kharpertian and Zareh Yaldizdjiyan for making me more sensitive to the Armenians' historical situation, and to Rose Garabedian for help with a number of Armenian terms. For their understanding and kindness I am obligated to Frederick I. Carpenter, Betty Rahv, and Robert Setrakian of the William Saroyan Foundation. I am indebted to the interlibrary loan service at Forbes Library in Northampton, Massachusetts, and at the Stevens Institute of Technology, as well as to the Columbia University

Library and the New York Public Library. But above all, I am grateful to Elaine and Katherine and John. Who know why.

Notes

1. Percy Lubbock, *The Craft of Fiction* (London: Jonathan Cape, 1921), 122.

2. According to Werner Sollors (*Beyond Ethnicity: Consent and Descent in American Culture* [New York: Oxford University Press, 1986], 25.), the term *ethnicity* was first used in 1941. The term *ethnic* is older, but Saroyan used the words *race* and *racial*. (See, for example, William Saroyan, "Seventy Thousand Assyrians," *The Daring Young Man on the Flying Trapeze and Other Stories* [New York: Random House, 1934], 32, and his introduction to *Hairenik: 1934–1939*, ed. Reuben Darbinian [Boston: Hairenik Press, 1939], xv.) Because these latter words now suggest meanings Saroyan did not intend, *ethnic* and *ethnicity* have been adopted for this volume.

3. James Joyce, *A Portrait of the Artist as a Young Man* (New York: Viking Press, 1964), 253.

4. Lawrence Lipton, *The Holy Barbarians* (New York: Grove Press, 1959), 232.

5. Weldon Kees, "Three Books," *Reviews and Essays: 1936–55*, ed. James Reidel (Ann Arbor: University of Michigan Press, 1988), 29. The review was originally published in 1938.

Acknowledgments

Nona Balakian's "The World of William Saroyan" is reprinted by permission of Macmillan Publishing Co. from her *Critical Encounters: Literary Views and Reviews, 1953–1977*. © 1978 by Nona Balakian.

Zori Balayan's "Arguments for Soviet Power . . ." is reprinted by permission of *Soviet Literature* from *Soviet Literature* 12 (357) (1977): 160–66. © 1977 by *Soviet Literature*.

Frederick I. Carpenter's "The Time of William Saroyan's Life" is reprinted by permission of American Council of Learned Societies from *Pacific Spectator* 1 (Winter 1947): 88–96. Copyright 1947 by the Pacific Coast Committee for the Humanities.

Excerpts from *William Saroyan: My Real Work Is Being*, by David Stephen Calonne. © 1983 by the University of North Carolina Press. Reprinted by permission.

Excerpts from William J. Fisher's "Whatever Happened to Saroyan?" are reprinted by permission of the National Council of Teachers of English from *College English* 16 (March 1955): 337. © 1955 by the National Council of Teachers of English.

Excerpts from Howard R. Floan's *William Saroyan* are reprinted by permission of Twayne Publishers, a division of G. K. Hall & Co., Boston, from his *William Saroyan*. © 1966 by Twayne Publishers, Inc.

Harry Keyishian's "The Dark Side of Saroyan" is reprinted by permission of Harry Keyishian from *Ararat: A Quarterly* 25 (Spring 1984): 47–49. © 1884 by the Armenian General Benevolent Union.

Excerpts from Harry Keyishian's "Michael Arlen and William Saroyan: Armenian Ethnicity and the Writer" are reprinted by permission of Associated University Presses from *The Old Century and the New: Essays in Honor of Charles Angoff*, edited by Alfred Rosa. © 1978 by Associated University Presses, Inc.

Philip Rahv's "Narcissus" is reprinted by permission of Betty T. Rahv from *Partisan Review* 2 (June 1935): 84–85.

William Saroyan's "Antranik of Armenia" is reprinted by permission of the William Saroyan Foundation from his *Inhale and Exhale* (New York: Random House, 1936).

Acknowledgments

Excerpts from William Saroyan's introduction to *Hairenik: 1934–1939* are reprinted by permission of the Hairenik Association, Inc.

William Saroyan's preface to his *The Daring Young Man on the Flying Trapeze and Other Stories* (New York: Random House, 1934) is reprinted by permission of the William Saroyan Foundation.

Part 1

THE SHORT FICTION

The Daring Young Man

The Armenian Church of the Holy Cross was built more than 1,000 years ago on the island of Akhtamar near the southern shore of Lake Van in eastern Anatolia. Akhtamar was a major religious center for the Armenian kingdom, and the church is one of the great achievements of Armenian art. Sculpted on the exterior walls are biblical scenes and pictures of animals that Noah brought onto the ark. Most of these images radiate a serene beauty and innocence in every way at odds with the hostile and belligerent world that has surrounded them for centuries.

The church was constructed during one of the few periods when Armenians were undisputed rulers of the region, but even then the landlocked kingdom was repeatedly attacked, and eventually it fell to Muhammadan invaders, the Ottoman Turks, who ruled until early in this century.[1] According to legend, Noah's ark came to rest on Ararat, a mountain 100 miles northeast of Akhtamar, and the story of Noah must have had special significance for Armenians under the Ottomans. Just as God had destroyed the wicked and saved only Noah and his family, so might He someday save His Christian people from their Islamic rulers. There was reason for the serenity expressed in the images at Akhtamar.

On the eastern shore of the lake are the ruins of Van Castle and the old city of Van, once the center of an Armenian kingdom. In 1915 this was the site of one of the fiercest battles in the Turkish War of Independence. Before the war more than 15,000 Armenians lived here among Turks and Kurds. Afterward only the shells of mosques and churches and acres and acres of ruined stores and houses remained. There were no Armenians alive.

From the castle, one still looks down on the ruins of the city and across the lake to the Church of the Holy Cross. The extremes of, on the one hand, a culture that ended in unimaginable horror and, on the other, images of sweet innocence, beauty, and charm suggest the moral and emotional dimensions of the world evoked in the stories of William Saroyan.

3

Saroyan might write about a Greek sailor or an Italian shop owner or an Armenian farmer, but his narrators almost always speak with a sensibility that is identifiably Armenian. For Saroyan the narrative was never as important as the way it was told. What mattered were nuances of attitude and feeling, essentially lyric qualities, revealed in the course of the telling.

Saroyan's Armenian sensibility can be felt clearly in "The Daring Young Man on the Flying Trapeze," one of his first published stories.[2] It originally appeared in a 1933 issue of *Story* magazine, where it attracted much attention, and, as the title story of his first book, published the next year, it made him famous. It is perhaps still the story for which he is best known.

"The Daring Young Man" very clearly announces a new presence in American literature, and that presence is Armenian. Although the word *Armenian* never appears in the story and an Armenian sensibility is never directly asserted, it can be felt everywhere. The story embodies an attitude toward experience that is unlike anything in earlier American fiction.

The story opens with the dreams and reveries of a young writer as he wakes into the morning world. His dreams, he feels, are what matter; everything else is something through which he must pass on his way back to the greater, visionary reality. But on this morning many of his dreams deal with tyranny, destruction, and loss. He thinks of the fall of Jericho and Rome, Charlie Chaplin in tears, Stalin and Hitler. The writers whom the young man remembers as he begins his day are the realists Flaubert and Maupassant. This day will not be a passage back to private visions. His dreams this morning are the material out of which the next few hours will be formed. They will be lived in intense awareness of the real and will bring all his dreams to an end.

The young writer has no great pretensions or ambitions. He wants only to be left alone with his words and ideas. He makes few demands of the world, and the world is indifferent to him. But the country is now in a depression, and he has no job, money, or food. He is not needed by anyone, and although he hopes eventually to find work, there is nothing he can do to support himself.

It occurs to him (but without seeming at all strange) that what he should do today is apply for the right to live, and so he walks to the local YMCA, where there is free paper and ink, and works for an hour on his application. Suddenly feeling faint, he leaves, gets some water, and goes to the library, where he reads Proust for a while. Again feeling faint, he goes home and carefully polishes and examines a penny he earlier found on the street. The penny, he notes, was minted in 1923, when the economy was still strong, and on the back are the words "In God We Trust Liberty." Lying on his bed, he envisions a city in flames. The earth seems to move away from him, and, knowing exactly what is about to happen to him but regretting nothing, he dies.

A "social realist" might have turned the story into a political statement, an indictment of social or economic injustice, but there is no indignation or anger in Saroyan's version. The political implications are obvious: America, however much it celebrates individualism, no longer has room for those who cannot fit into the system. But this point is incidental to Saroyan's purpose, for what interests him most is how the young man can survive as long as he does in a world that is indifferent or even hostile to him.

The young man is strangely euphoric in spite of what is happening. He is magically graceful and free. To be angry and see the world as an enemy would mean sacrificing the right to live in private visions and dreams. He feels no self-pity, only pleasure in his books, dreams, and ideas. He suffers, and yet he is never unhappy. His sadness is a pleasant melancholy.

Saroyan's politics are utterly fatalistic, but behind them are centuries in which Armenians had lived with little political authority. Although in his complete independence the daring young man may initially seem like Thoreau, life at Walden was a political act; Thoreau was doing something for others to imitate. The daring young man, however, does not see himself as a model for others; he wants only to be left alone, and his reward is his freedom.

The daring young man never has to agree with someone or do what someone else wants. But his freedom is solipsistic and made possible only by retreating from the world or moving through it like a ghost. He is a specter and a spectator; he speaks to no one, and no one speaks to him.

The story should be read as a parable of Armenia and its survival through centuries of oppression. Armenians rarely offered military or physical resistance, but in private they maintained a literature and tradition to which their conquerors had little or no access. A complex epic poem entitled *David of Sassoun* was, for example, handed down in secret from generation to generation. The survival of the work, which imagines an Armenian victory over Islam, is astonishing. Since the Ottomans would have considered it treasonous, it could not be written down; it had to be memorized. Yet the work was perfectly known throughout Armenia for hundreds of years. A number of different versions arose, and by the time scholars in the nineteenth century began to record them, the poem had become virtually a literature in itself—a complicated set of dream poems or visions about an impossible victory.

Those visions are like the dreams of the daring young man. What matters in the end is not success in the world, which would never be possible without unacceptable compromise, but the preservation of dreams themselves. More than endurance is involved, for the object is to remain, within one's self, untouched by oppression. The young man's survival is never achieved with bitterness or anger. There is no rage. He is not vindictive, and as a result his innocence and grace are never corrupted. Like the images at Akhtamar, he is isolated but serene in an appalling world.

It is worth noting here that in his writings Saroyan rarely attacked Turks or expressed animosity toward them. Not they, certainly, but the Ottoman government had been responsible for the Armenian horror. Saroyan's vision derives from Rousseau: governments and institutions, not people, are responsible for the evil in the world. In his stories Saroyan at times created situations that his critics considered sentimental, but the sentimentality freed him from the bitterness and anger he must have found among his Armenian friends and family. Like the daring young man, he found redemption in dreams.

To Saroyan's contemporaries, who thought they could end the depression with radical political and economic change, his gentle world in which people preserve themselves by cultivating inner sweetness seemed foolish and irresponsible. In an age that took its politics seriously Saroyan's stories seemed at best diversions or entertainments, and Saroyan himself was widely attacked by critics for not putting his talents to better use. "At the moment," wrote a critic for the *Nation*, "Mr. Saroyan is most of the things a serious artist is not. He is an exhibitionist, a verbalist, a poseur, a nose thumber, a prima donna, and a victim of genius mania."[3] Otis Ferguson in the *New Republic* concluded that readers would find "precious little" in Saroyan's book except "a posture, a performing young man on his typewriter keys."[4]

Saroyan was far more serious than his critics realized. The country was in political and economic turmoil, and his stories repeatedly suggest that ultimately there were no acceptable solutions. Moving just beneath the surface of all Saroyan's best stories is the certainty that oppression is inevitable, that there are no utopias except the ones we imagine for ourselves.

"The Daring Young Man on the Flying Trapeze" was originally the first story in Saroyan's collection of that name. Since that story had made him famous, it was logical to place it first. But its Armenian character is not explicit, and perhaps for that reason he followed it immediately with "Seventy Thousand Assyrians," in which his Armenian background is prominent. This story's importance to the collection (and to Saroyan's work generally) is suggested by the fact that when the book was reissued in 1964, he reshuffled the contents, placing "Seventy Thousand Assyrians" first and burying the title story two-thirds of the way into the volume.

"Seventy Thousand Assyrians" is the best story in the collection and more typical of Saroyan's work than "The Daring Young Man on the Flying Trapeze." The latter is a cut-down version of an unpublished novel, "Trapeze over the Universe," and its stream-of-consciousness technique and concern with the sensibility of a young artist are indebted, at least superficially, to James Joyce. As the opening paragraph suggests, however, the major influence on "Seventy Thousand Assyrians" is Sherwood Anderson, who taught Saroyan more about writing stories than anyone else did. Although Anderson's influence is discussed later in this volume, it should be noted here that he showed Saroyan it was possible to develop a unique "voice," and in "Seventy Thousand Assyrians" Saroyan began to speak in a manner unmistakably his own and to devise the kind of story for which he became famous—a "story," that is, that has to do less with the intricacies of character and plot than with the moods and feelings of the narrator.

In such stories very little may happen: what matters is the sound of the narrator speaking. "The short story form, as such, never appealed to me especially," Saroyan said. What he wanted was "to say the same words I was saying when I talked."[5] The short story was suitable for that purpose simply because it was "without a doubt the freest form of writing."[6] But even the short story traditionally implied limits, and what he wanted was a "form" he could stretch in any direction he wished. He found what he wanted "between the essay and the short story"—"a form or formlessness which would permit me to write" (*Assyrian*, xxiv). The model for that was Anderson's leisurely, digressive stories.

The man who narrates "Seventy Thousand Assyrians" is Armenian but says he doesn't know what that designation means any more than he knows what it means to be English or Japanese. When people ask him what his background is, he tells them, but he doesn't think it has any special importance. He says his uncle once made speeches to raise money for Armenians, victims first of war and then of a massive earthquake, yet in private seemed to feel only contempt toward man and God for all his people had suffered. He knew God had been unjust. To think of oneself as Armenian seemed to invite a general disgust or horror with life.

The story is set in San Francisco during the depression and is narrated by a writer who wants "to speak a more universal language. The heart of man, the unwritten part of man, that which is eternal and common to all races."[7] Having little money, he goes to a barbers' school to get a cheap haircut. The barber, Theodore Badal, is Assyrian, and as he talks about his family and his culture it becomes clear that Assyrians—of whom there are only 70,000 left—have suffered even more than Armenians. As far as the barber can see, there is no hope for the future of his people: all those who remain will die, be murdered by Arabs, or be absorbed into another culture. But the writer, as he walks home, thinks that in fact the Assyrian barber is in certain ways a greater man than those who outwardly have been more successful but whose lives have never been touched by grief so vast as that which Badal feels at the destruction of his people. Through his suffering, the Assyrian—like the narrator's uncle—has reached an understanding others do not have.

But Saroyan does not pursue the point. Instead he begins to talk about "the stuff that is eternal in man" (although he said a moment before that the barber has been destroyed "spiritually") and then adds a long digression in which it appears that Bardal in some unexplained fashion carries within himself the heritage of an ancient people (*Daring*, 40). This is followed by a plea for understanding and brotherhood, and the story ends in an air of high idealism, with Theodore Badal "standing in a barbershop, in San Francisco, in 1933, and being, still, himself, the whole race" (*Daring*, 41).

Earlier the narrator said he did "not believe in races" or "governments": the eternal aspects of humanity transcend these divisions and orders (*Daring*, 32). But Badal's suffering, which he shares with the rest of the world, arises from his identity as an Assyrian. To retreat into oneself and the sufferings of one's "race," the narrator has learned, is not solipsism but the means through which a common humanity is reached.

When Saroyan's stories succeed it is often because there is beneath the surface a painful vision—an Assyrian's sense that his culture will be destroyed, an Armenian's recognition that God is unjust. Despite this element, the narrators usually remain jaunty, good-humored, sweet—Saroyanesque.[8] In their exuberance they are like the daring young man, astonishingly graceful and free, but the reality of the world and its sufferings has been exposed. There is always the fear that these people will fall, and the stories make clear what waits for them when they do.

"Seventy Thousand Assyrians" shows Saroyan dealing with these emotional complexities better than he does anywhere else in the book, and it is some measure of the story's success that its admirers included writers as different as Budd Schulberg and J. D. Salinger, both of whom read it at the beginning of their careers. Salinger read it when it was first published in *Story* magazine and was very impressed, and his biographer, Ian Hamilton, named Saroyan (who in turn would admire *The Catcher in the Rye*) as an important influence on Salinger's work.[9] Schulberg remembered coming across "Seventy Thousand Assyrians" in 1934 and being astonished by what it managed to do: "It dared to be not only its own content but its own form. You will never know how difficult that is to do until you try it."[10]

Not all the stories in the book balance between lighthearted grace and underlying tragedy. One of the better pieces, "Aspirin Is a Member of the N.R.A.," is also among the bleakest of Saroyan's early stories. The narrator is a daring young man who fell, and his story is an unrelieved invective against American life. While many of Saroyan's stories written in the 1930s deal with sufferings brought on by the depression, none are as bitter. This one was drawn from Saroyan's personal anguish and loneliness during the six months he spent in New York City when he was 19, trying, with no success, to establish himself as a writer.

The story's narrator thinks his sufferings parallel the grief and pain he finds on the streets and in the subway, and he imagines a suffering nation using aspirin to deaden its pain. Aspirin *is* part of the National Recovery Act. But as he says, eventually if you take too much, it won't do its work anymore, and the story ends with an apocalyptic vision of people finally taking revenge, destroying the mechanical, inhuman world around them. It is a vision echoed in Nathanael West's *The Day of the Locust* and in the poetry of Lawrence Ferlinghetti and Allen Ginsberg.

Although "Aspirin Is a Member of the N.R.A." is the most directly political story in the book, it contains no solutions to the social problems it describes—or rather it suggests there are no solutions except those an individual works out for him- or herself. The narrator can respond only with his rage, and yet the fact that he can do at least that much must have been crucial for Saroyan. The ability, indeed the right, to express anger at authority was conventionally denied Armenians under the Ottomans. In "Aspirin Is a Member of the N.R.A." Saroyan talks about his father (a writer, too), who went to jail for protesting the way his people were treated and who then had to desert his homeland since, having spoken so openly, his life was now in danger.

A New Kind of Fiction

When he was 14 Saroyan read the stories of Guy de Maupassant, and they "put [him] to work in earnest." One might expect he would have been most interested in the way the stories are designed, since Maupassant was above all a master craftsman. But what Saroyan admired was their emotional world—the powerful "sadness" they evoked. That sadness, he said, "contained within itself a power and joyousness which I believed to be more important to me than anything else in the world that I might discover, inherit, earn, or steal."[11] In turn, in his own stories Saroyan was concerned primarily with stating or expressing emotion.

It has been said that the short story has stronger affinities with lyric poetry than with novels.[12] The novel may present greater possibilities for analyzing complex social relations, but the short story can be especially effective if it focuses on matters of private or at least personal emotion. The distinction, while clearly not absolute, can be useful in understanding Saroyan's objectives. Certainly his fiction is closer to the poetry of Walt Whitman and William Carlos Williams than, say, to the novels of Henry James.

As mentioned earlier, no one had a greater influence on Saroyan than Sherwood Anderson, who in effect tried to do in fiction what Williams and Whitman did in poetry. Williams and Whitman did not want to abolish form, as some of their critics have claimed; rather, they wanted form to arise naturally from what they said. Both were, in this radical sense, formalists, discovering new limits, new shapes for their art. Their opposite was Edgar Allan Poe, for whom the story or poem was an exercise within imposed limits. In the poem those limits included meter, rhyme, traditional form, and so forth; in fiction plot was the principal structuring device. Both Whitman and Williams were able to subvert Poe's aesthetics in poetry. Whitman created a verse line that produced its own inner tension with little or no reference to conventional metrics, and Williams, in such works as *Kora in Hell*, created "poems" that, shaped as paragraphs, owed nothing to traditional prosody and thereby called into question conventional assumptions about what poems were supposed to do.

Anderson's revolution was less sweeping but no less influential. First, he made narrative subordinate to what he called "tone," by which he meant the general feeling or attitude the work conveyed. To accomplish this, he imagined a new relationship between the writer and language. Words were not merely a means through which the story could be told; they were, he believed, the direct expression of the narrator, whose narrative was in turn effectively a pretext for expressing subjective attitudes and responses. Stories were therefore to be shaped primarily not by the requirements of plot but by an indigenous "form" that involved the expression of "tone" or subjective feeling in its subtle variations. Form derived from "the materials of the tale and the teller's reaction to them."¹³

One of Anderson's most frequently anthologized stories, for example, is "Death in the Woods," originally published in 1926. It concerns an elderly woman mistreated by her son and her husband. The family has little money, and her greatest problem is finding food for them and their farm animals. One winter's day, she goes to get food in the town, and, on the way home, in an isolated, snow-covered clearing, she dies. Her dogs circle round, waiting until they are certain she is dead, then feast on the food she was bringing them.

The story is less important for its narrative, however, than for the way it is told. The narrator was a boy when the woman died, and he was among those who saw her body in the snow. That image has been with him for many years, and slowly he has constructed a context for it. He says there had been another story to explain what happened but that one had not satisfied him, and so he felt it necessary to construct what seemed to him the authentic version.

In fact, however, there is much in his story that the narrator could not know for certain. Essentially he has constructed his story out of his own experiences and things he heard when growing up. He describes, for example, the way in which the dogs come up and look in the dying woman's face. He says he knows this happened because once he was in a similar circumstance, but in fact what he says is at best speculation. Anderson's point, of course, is that it doesn't matter whether a story like this is factually accurate. What does matter is the narrator's psychology; the story is about his obsession with a past he cannot really know.

Saroyan studied Anderson's work closely, and to understand the aesthetic assumptions behind stories like "Seventy Thousand Assyrians" it is important to understand the expressionist tradition in which Anderson worked. Although Saroyan himself worked from time to time in other traditions, he never abandoned expressionist aesthetics completely.

James Schevill pointed out many years ago that "much of the confusion about Anderson's work may be traced to the false belief that he was a naturalistic writer."[14] Critics have read Anderson's work as if he were concerned primarily with character and plot, and since he handled neither consistently well, the critical judgment has often been unfavorable.[15] To understand Anderson's achievement, it is crucial to recognize first that his words always appear to be *spoken*. He was a storyteller for whom the story was less important than the way it was told, and his prose should be "heard" as well as "read."

Anderson said he originally learned how to tell stories by listening to his father, but his most important teacher was Gertrude Stein. In *A Story Teller's Story* (1924) he wrote that he had been excited by Stein's series of experiments in nonreferential language in her book *Tender Buttons* (1914). Words, as Stein showed, could live in a universe of their own making; they were more than signs, more than a way of indicating a world distinct from both the writer and the audience (Anderson, 359, 362). In conversation with a painter sometime later, Anderson realized that brushstrokes could be seen as the direct expression of the artist. Together that realization and Stein's practice led to Anderson's conviction that language could be used not merely to describe or define but to express the self much as color did in a painting. In a 1934 essay defending Stein he concluded, "The world of art, of any art, is never the real world. . . . There is a world outside of reality being created. The object is not to be true to the world of reality but to the world outside reality."[16]

In his own work Anderson rarely built a verbal universe as abstract and nonreferential as Stein did in, for example, *Stanzas in Meditation*. What he did was take this new sense of the potential of language and use it to express an essentially midwestern, populist, and often-sentimental view of life that had to do less with Turgenev and Chekhov (despite what some of his more enthusiastic defenders liked to believe) than with Edward Howe and Hamlin Garland. The Midwest in his fiction is much the same as the one they recorded, but it is expressed in terms of Anderson's sensibility and the sensibilities of his narrators.

Stein understood exactly what Anderson was doing. In her review of *A Story Teller's Story* she wrote that Anderson's business was to "express life," not to "reflect," "describe," "embroider," or "photograph" it.[17] The significant word is *express*, which links Anderson to Gottfried Benn, August Stramm, Wassily Kandinsky, Oskar Kokoschka, and other writers, artists, and composers associated with the German expressionist movement.[18] Stein was identifying her disciple as a writer of international, rather than merely regional or American, interest.

On the one hand, "'Expressionism,'" according to R. S. Furness, "is a descriptive term which has to cover so many disparate cultural manifestations as to be virtually meaningless." Nonetheless, the movement had in common "everywhere the call . . . for self-expression, creativity, ecstatic fervour and a ruthless denial of tradition."[19] There was also a deep distrust of mimetic art, particularly late nineteenth-century realism and naturalism. The subjective sources of art were not only acknowledged but privileged. An expressionist refused simply to imitate the surrounding world; his art had its origin and power within, and externality was valued primarily as material out of which an image or expression of the subjective could be shaped. As Roger Asselineau has written, "*Ex*pressionism essentially consists in *ex*teriorizing subjective *im*pressions by *ex*aggerating certain aspects of *ex*ternal reality," and "this is precisely what Sherwood Anderson does in some of his stories."[20]

Saroyan studied the work of his master closely and in some ways improved on it and followed its implications further. Anderson tended, for example, to speak through masks or to use narrators (as in "Death in the Woods"), but as Asselineau has indicated, the expressionist's principal resources are subjective and personal. Saroyan at times also used narrators other than himself (as when he used dialect, an approach he may have taken from Ring Lardner rather than Anderson), but essentially he spoke in his own voice, taking his story in whatever direction the moment seemed to require. The world and its language were no more than material from which to evoke an image of his internal self.

Saroyan's willingness to ignore all the conventions of storytelling is clear in the pieces collected in *The Daring Young Man on the Flying Trapeze*. Most of these "stories" are in effect monologues. In "Sleep in Unheavenly Peace," for example, Saroyan talks about San Francisco at night—its neon-lighted streets and its movie theaters, restaurants, prostitutes, and derelicts. "A Cold Day" is about the weather, the author's books, his phonograph, and America. "Love, Death, Sacrifice, and So Forth" is about a scene in a movie. "And Man" is about adolescence. In "A Curved Line" he talks about a visit to an art class. In "Myself upon the Earth" Saroyan summaries the aesthetic assumption underlying all these works: "Do you know that I do not believe there is really such a thing as a poem-form, a story-form or a novel-form? I believe there is man only. . . . I am trying to carry over into this story of mine the man that I am. And as much of my earth as I am able" (*Daring*, 58).

"The Shepherd's Daughter," the last story in the book, reaches this conclusion from another direction. In this story Saroyan's grandmother uses a fable to teach him (or to try to teach him) a moral, but he remains unconvinced—though he obviously enjoys the story and admires the way his grandmother has told it.

Eventually, Saroyan pursued the implications of expressionism into linguistic abstractions that blur the traditional lines between prose fiction and other genres and that anticipate the work of Jack Kerouac and language-centered writers like Clark Coolidge. Possibly Saroyan was led into these more experimental stories through the work and theoretical writings of his close friend Hilaire Hiler, a San Francisco painter who later settled in Paris as a member of the expatriate community. Saroyan contributed an essay to Hiler's introduction to expressionist theory, *Why Abstract?* (1936), in which he argues that "a strong emotional feeling is the basis of all art expression."[21] In his own work Hiler followed Kandinsky by realizing that expression solely in terms of abstract form and color. Similarly, Saroyan eventually experimented with abstract, nonreferential patterns of language.

But in most of his work Saroyan never deviated far from Anderson's example. Even Saroyan's prose style, although distinctively his own, can be traced to Anderson. There was, said Anderson, "a certain music to all good prose writing. There is tone and color in words as in notes of music,"[22] and for him that music was found in the spoken language, specifically the phrasings, rhythms, and idioms of the Midwest he had known as a child. Saroyan's diction is similarly musical, although drawn from very different sources. In particular, his English incorporates the jazzlike rhythms and sharp tempos he found in San Francisco in the 1920s and early 1930s. He walked around the city, listening carefully and absorbing the spoken language until it had merged into a voice distinctly his own.[23]

In 1976, 35 years after Anderson's death and very near the end of his own career, Saroyan wrote that *A Story Teller's Story* had taught him his most important lesson: "that which is under your nose, that is your subject." "I acknowledge his influence," Saroyan concluded, "and am beholden to him."[24]

Anderson's influence was not always for the best. However modern he seemed even among the American expatriates in Paris, he was always imaginatively more comfortable in the small-town Midwest. There is something provincial about many of his stories, and the same can be said of Saroyan's. Whereas Anderson is most at home in the small-town Midwest, Saroyan's achievement lies in re-creations of his native Fresno, California.

To his contemporaries, Anderson's stories seemed daring and modern not only in their technique but also in their frank attitudes toward sex. Yet their tone could be adolescent and self-indulgent. He and his narrators were often narcissistic, nostalgic, or sentimental when they were supposed to be insightful or profound. Although the stories often deal with social injustice, they rarely offer a meaningful solution. The same is true of Saroyan's.

Anderson's stories are too concerned with the narrator's sensibility to confront economic or social matters objectively. George Willard, the central figure in Anderson's best-known work, *Winesburg, Ohio* (1919), is an adolescent aware of the emotionally impoverished life of his village but has no answer for it and, at the end of the book, leaves to start a new life in the city. That sort of conclusion is exactly what one would expect from an aesthetic position that argued against close, objective scrutiny of social and political problems. The writer did not work by conscious design; an understanding of economic injustice required the kind of analysis and objectivity that expressionism specifically rejected.

Similarly, expressionism rejected any formal critical standard, and an author had no objective way to distinguish qualitatively between stories. Even Anderson's best collections, such as *The Triumph of the Egg* (1921), contain what some readers must feel are weak, ephemeral pieces beside some of his most emotionally complex and intriguing stories.

The same faults are found repeatedly in Saroyan, for whom mere self-expression could be indistinguishable from art. Even some of his best stories, such as "Seventy Thousand Assyrians," shift suddenly from complex emotion and insight to the great Saroyanesque ideals, which, given the nature of his aesthetics, never have to be tested against experience. In short, conviction and testimony replace analysis and reflection. Saroyan could use his fiction to complain about injustices in American life without ever having to come to terms with political and economic realities.

Not surprisingly, Saroyan suffered considerable criticism from the Left, but he, like Anderson, found his strongest critics among the formalists.

In 1921, when Anderson's reputation was at its peak, Percy Lubbock published *The Craft of Fiction*, arguing for the kind of self-conscious, objective craftsmanship that shaped the works of Henry James. Lubbock argued above all that the writer was not part of the story. He or she should be invisible like the puppet master behind the screen, allowing the story to reveal itself, rather than stand in front of the stage telling his audience what was happening.[25]

For many years Lubbock's ideas marked a major division between writers and critics: on the one hand, there were formalists (generally critics such as Lubbock), and, on the other, there were expressionists (generally writers such as Anderson, Faulkner, Saroyan, and Wolfe). Even among expressionists Saroyan was obviously extreme, seemingly publishing everything except his checkbook and laundry lists, and as a result, he was treated with special fury and scorn by the critics. The very years in which he wrote his best short fiction were those in which he could not get a fair critical hearing.

Lubbock's standards were obviously restrictive. They not only narrowed the writer's possibilities but also provided critics and readers with theoretically "objective" criteria to judge fiction. Saroyan could not hope for serious consideration in such company. What could they say to a writer who set out to write a book of short stories in a month?

That was exactly what he did. After selling "The Daring Young Man" (for $15) in December 1933[26] he decided to write a story a day, and by the end of January he had completed his first book. That enormous productivity in turn set the pattern for most of his early work, which was often written with little preparation and little or no revision. He became virtually a writing factory and by the end of the decade had completed 500 stories as well as dozens of essays, poems, and plays, the most famous of which, *The Time of Your Life*, was written in six days. "Everything . . . is a little too much," Saroyan said. "Except for me and Thomas Wolfe."[27]

This sheer quantity is the key both to Saroyan's best work and at least in part to his commercial success. The major stories depend on a sense of immediacy and spontaneity, and that could easily be destroyed by excessive revision. Eventually he developed a type of story that he knew would find an audience and that he could write quickly. It rapidly developed a situation and two or three characters. There were no great emotional arcs, as in the early work. The tone might be genial or sad but never tragic.

But the early work, typed out as soon as it came to him, retained its urgency, freshness, and immediacy. He never revised the stories in his first three books and in fact felt "it was dishonest to do so" (*After Thirty Years*, 19). He believed the writer should be possessed by the writing itself; the movement of the language, not the writer's intentions, should be in charge. What he wanted was a written language as fluid and natural as the language he heard in the street. A story, he said, was "the most natural of forms, coming directly from people talking to one another . . . long before writing . . . long before literature." Ideally, then, a story would try to maintain the illusion that it was spoken. "The nearer [writing] comes to a approximation of real talk," he said, "The better [it] is" (*After Thirty Years*, 95, 107).

Linda W. Wagner has argued that "much of what occurs in literature today" is an outgrowth of an aesthetic ideal deeply rooted in American literature: "the creation through language of the individual speaking voice."[28] That "individual speaking voice" is frequently the author's, and authorial presence has often been deeply criticized. According to Oscar Wilde, for example, "Man is least himself when he talks in his own person. Give him a mask and he will tell you the truth."[29] Saroyan, on the other hand, would have argued that a successful story derives its power and veracity directly from the author. In answer to an interviewer who asked him what "the form of [his] most characteristic literary work" was, Saroyan replied that it was he himself.[30]

"By making fiction voice-centered," as Michael Stephens says in *The Dramaturgy of Style: Voice in Short Fiction*, "the stress goes away from representational toward the presentational."[31] As a result, in Charles Olson's words, *"That which exists through itself is what is called the meaning."*[32] The story, that is, lies in the modulations of the voice, expressing (rather than merely stating or showing) a moment of feeling or sensibility. What matters most, as Stephens writes, is to be "faithful to the rhythms of experience" (Stephens, 5).

Short fiction is particularly suited for this kind of writing. It can be difficult, for example, to sustain expressionistic intensity over great periods of time, and as the writer's moods change so must the tone and quality of the fiction. Saroyan, though he tried to write novels, was never very successful at doing so, and the only one for which he is known, *The Human Comedy,* is really a series of interrelated stories. His autobiographical works were sufficiently general in plan to allow for sudden shifts in mood, and as we will see, they are in some respects closer to collections of short stories than to conventional memoirs.

A short story, on the other hand—at least the kind of short story Saroyan chose to write—could be finished in one or two sittings. There were no rules except those which emerged in the writing. The work defined itself.

The Expressionist

Saroyan's second book, *Inhale and Exhale,* published less than two years after his first, contains 71 essays and stories. Although he wanted to include more, his publisher objected, and the rest appeared a few months later in *Three Times Three.* Both books contain excellent work, but neither was particularly popular with either the critics or the public. Although the first printing of *Inhale and Exhale* sold well (perhaps because *The Daring Young Man* had been so well received), the second was largely ignored. And *Three Times Three,* published by a small press, never had a wide distribution.

Saroyan by this time was accustomed to large royalty checks, however, and, a compulsive gambler, he was now often in need of money. Much of his later work, such as *The Human Comedy,* may in part have been written simply for a market and for money; nevertheless, the author of *Inhale and Exhale* and *Three Times Three* was still confident that he did not need to compromise his work in order to reach a large audience.

Inhale and Exhale is one of Saroyan's major achievements, a book of enormous variety and drive—really nine "books" in one, for the 438 pages of small type are divided into nine sections, each of which might stand on its own. Perhaps the book's formidable length was one reason it was poorly received, although several years later when Saroyan tried publishing a version with only 31 of the stories, it too failed to attract much attention.

Some of the stories, such as "The Revolution" and "Solemn Advice to a Young Man about to Accept Undertaking as a Profession," are modeled on works by Ring Lardner, those in which narrators reveal, by the way they talk, a good deal more about themselves than they may think they do. Such stories in *Inhale and Exhale* are about self-deception, but most of the other stories in the book, following Anderson's example, are involved with self-discovery or self-expression.

Some of the pieces are slight. Most of the "stories" in the section titled "A Tipped Hat to the Lamp Post" are, for example, no more than brief sketches, and the final section, "The Little Dog Laughed to See Such Sport," comprises brief journalistic pieces about Saroyan's first visit to the Soviet Union. The stories in "The Gay and Melancholy Flux" and "Yea and Amen," many of which are drawn from Saroyan's childhood, are more interesting, although at times they are overburdened with calculated whimsy. In "Our Friends the Mice," for example, the narrator's older brother removes the cheese from his family's mousetraps, puts it beside them on the floor, and tells everybody that some mice are simply smarter than others and know about going around to the back, avoiding the spring.

The Daring Young Man had for Saroyan been a test of skill, a book that had been written, or rather typed, quickly; had sold well; and had included at least one story, "Seventy Thousand Assyrians," that was highly regarded. The pressure behind the stories in *Inhale and Exhale* was quite different. Saroyan was now confident of his abilities and focused intently on the subjects he would pursue throughout his career: his memories of his boyhood, his ideas about writing, and above all his sense of ethnic identity. All three subjects could be found in *The Daring Young Man*; in *Inhale and Exhale*, however, they became his central and nearly exclusive concerns.

"Everything," said Saroyan at the beginning of his book, "begins with inhale and exhale, and never ends."[33] The form of each story, he wrote, "is the form of myself, my own breathing." To write was to talk—to "inhale and exhale": "the greatest writing is the most conversational, the least artful" (*Inhale*, 245). Everything seemed to depend on the moment of composition, the way the writer felt as he put the words down on paper.

In "Panorama Unmerciful" he said that he couldn't help but write and that after he had written a certain number of words, he had a story. But the professors told him all stories must follow three rules. He didn't know or care about rules; he kept on writing, and whatever came out was "precisely what it is . . . and let the professors jump in the river" (*Inhale*, 378).

Saroyan's stories modulate through a complex series of emotions caught in the rhythms of the language, the sounds of the words, and the excitement, passion, or despair in the breath of the man who speaks and writes. At times this quality leads to passages of great beauty:

"The house was locked, dark sullen, myself inside and my brother there, and in the yard the tall eucalyptus tree was black, quieter than a pebble, unbirded, in the deep pool of night, the porch of the house staring openly at my fear, the windows mocking it, no one inside, myself in the street, the whole earth empty, and every heart turned inward to secret.

There is no place to turn, I said. (*Inhale*, 29)

Graceful yet emotionally complex passages like this appear throughout the book, and at their best the stories are an intricate weave of feeling and language. Their cadences are at times syncopated, nervous, and jazzlike, as in the following passage from "Six Hundred and Sixty-six": "My father, an alien, walked through the streets of New York, Good morning, Ben. Good morning, I said. The train shot forward and he sat at the window, looking at America. The germ of my life leapt at his heart and he said, I will go where the sun is and build a house there and breathe my life" (*Inhale*, 273).

Other works, such as "World Wilderness of Time Lost," move with euphoria and grace ("If I walk into the day smiling I will live and the wilderness of the world will grow into a garden before the clearness of my glance" [*Inhale*, 114]). The language in "Antranik of Armenia," which is about a famous Armenian general, mixes high lyricism and elegy, celebrating Armenian identity while mourning the fact that Armenia as a country is gone. The story is in part sentimental, but sentimentality here becomes a way of dealing with terrible suffering—as, for that matter, does the lyrical sweep of the language: "And the sadness of Armenia, my country, was so great in me that, sitting in the automobile, returning to Erivan, the only thing I could remember about Armenia was the quiet way General Antranik talked with my uncle many years ago and the tears in my uncle's eyes when he was gone, and the painful way my uncle's lips were twisting" (*Inhale*, 265).

"The Black Tartars" is narrated in a comparatively subdued and factual manner, but its effect, dependent largely on the words *live greatly*, is powerful (*Inhale*, 397, 405). There is nothing sentimental, as in "Antranik of Armenia," or insistently idealistic, as in "Seventy Thousand Assyrians." Saroyan works here in a very different range of tone and feeling and does so with great skill.

The narrator says that on a train from Kiev to Kharkov he met a man named Karachi, one of 10 Black Tartars left in Russia. Nine years earlier there had been a dozen Black Tartars, including Karachi's brother, Mago, the man who "would live greatly." To him, living greatly meant the survival of his people, and he chose as his wife a Black Tartar named Komi. To prove he loved her, he stole first a horse, then a dress, and finally an American car belonging to the government. To steal a car like that, Karachi says, "is to die," and Mago was brought to trial, protesting that he had done the deed only to prove his love. The judge, however, let Mago go, but then one day Mago "saw Komi in an automobile with the Judge. The Judge was crowding over Komi, and Komi was laughing at him." Mago broke into her house and, "kissing her lips and hands and hair," tied her up, carried her away to the mountains, and murdered her: "He did not want her to live if she would not love him" (*Inhale*, 399). Nothing is said about Mago's fate except that there are now only 10 Black Tartars left. Karachi at the end explains what his brother did by saying he "wanted to live greatly."

The story, like "Seventy Thousand Assyrians," is about a defeated people and the horrors that overtake them ("Capitalist, Fascist, or proletarian, it is the same everywhere" [*Inhale*, 399]). "Living greatly" means living as a Black Tartar (or Armenian or Assyrian); nothing is more important. No one seems to condemn Mago; the murder is not defended, but Karachi tries to explain it away, saying, "A man must love deeply to do such a thing" (*Inhale*, 405). Karachi's explanation is wrong, or at least only partly true, however, since he doesn't care about his heritage ("He would rather be a Russian, anyway" [*Inhale*, 397]) and so doesn't see that his brother's act is more than a crime of passion. If Mago's people are not to survive, then he, rather than an official from the government, will control fate.

"The Black Tartars" also concerns Saroyan's ideas about language and the way he wanted to use it. Karachi tells the story, but since he can't speak English, a Jewish girl on the train has to translate for the narrator and, in turn, the reader. At one point the judge asks Mago what language he speaks, and he lists Arabic, Kurdish, Russian, and Turkish but adds that when he uses words from these languages, they become Black Tartar words: "any words we use are in our language" (*Inhale*, 402). What Karachi says can be translated; what matters is what he says, not the way he says it. Mago, on the other hand, *is* the language he speaks, whatever language that should be. Saroyan would have said the same about his stories: the writer and his words are inseparable.

Most of Saroyan's collections of short fiction contain at least one piece in which he presents his theories of writing. The most sustained example of such a piece in *Inhale and Exhale* is "Poem, Story, Novel." This essay begins as a parody of Gertrude Stein but then becomes a

serious formulation of the aesthetic ideas Saroyan had developed from
Anderson. The *authentic* Stein, to quote from her essay on "Poetry and
Grammar," sounds like this: "They had their names and naturally I
called them by the names they had and in doing so having begun looking at them I called them by their names with passion and that made
poetry, I did not mean it to make poetry but it did, it made the Tender
Buttons, and the Tender Buttons was very good poetry it made a lot
more poetry, and I will now more and more tell about that and how it
happened."[34]

Saroyan's parody in the opening paragraph of "Poem, Story, Novel"
has the nervous repetition characteristic of Stein's prose: "A poem is
of course, is: it merely is, and it is so named, a poem: a thing and an
unthing, something: always it is afterwards and seldom before, coming
when and never coming while, which is a difference, and a poem is a
difference: an affair of now, from an affair of then."[35]

Stein at this time was enjoying a considerable celebrity. She had
published a best-seller, *The Autobiography of Alice B. Toklas*, in 1933,
and the following year her opera with music by Virgil Thomson, *Four
Saints in Three Acts*, had been produced and well received. She had also
recently completed a successful lecture tour (during which she met
with Saroyan twice), and her lectures, including "Poetry and Grammar," had been published as *Lectures in America* in 1935. She was a
person of much importance in the literary world, but, Saroyan thought,
"She was just a little boring for a swift new writer."[36]

Certainly most of Saroyan's readers would have recognized the parody at the beginning of "Poem, Story, and Novel"; one didn't have to
be a great writer or a close reader to catch Stein's distinctive rhythms
and mannerisms. But for some reason, which is not clear from the piece
itself, Saroyan suddenly switched from parody to a serious statement
of his own expressionist aesthetics. Perhaps because of his dislike of
revision or simply out of carelessness, he let the opening sentences
stand, inappropriate though they now were, and went on to define
what, aside from the obvious differences, he felt distinguishes short
fiction from poems and novels.

He insisted first that a poem is a kind of absolute reality, complete
in itself (Stein had argued in her lectures that poems had to do with
naming). A poem begins and ends in itself—as, to use Saroyan's met-
aphor, does the sun (*Inhale*, 286). A story, on the other hand, he
believed, is like a dream, making connections and relationships

throughout all the disparate events of experience. A story, then, is not created or put together like a machine but simply occurs, as dreams do. A story isn't intended to explain or give meaning to events; it is, he thought, its own end and purpose.

A story, furthermore, begins outside language and is then realized by the author in language: "It is the articulated word of an ancient wordlessness" (*Inhale*, 287). The author finds the story within him- or herself. It does not arise from a social need, and it has nothing to do with politics. Any desire to "bring about" stories was to be resisted, he thought; they must arise of themselves. Saroyan's advice to a young writer would be "to take language not from language itself but from silence and from one's self" (*Inhale*, 288).

A novel, in turn, is only a context of stories held together by the fact of a single awareness: the writer's. Otherwise, any work of long fiction could be only a construction, its order something imposed. One of the greatest novels ever written, Saroyan argued, was the journal of Henri Frédéric Amiel (1821–81), which he had first read many years before in an abridged version and which had recently been published in an expanded edition. Amiel's "novel" arose from the fact of his having simply got himself, in his multiple complexities, on paper.[37] The book did not arise from any preconceived notion about character or plot or from any sense of what a work of art should accomplish; it was simply the daily record or expression of one man, its unity lying in the singularity of his vision.

The only novel greater than Amiel's journal, Saroyan believed, was Joyce's *Ulysses*. Yet it was probably not Joyce's careful craftmanship that led Saroyan to give the honor to *Ulysses* but rather its use of stream of consciousness—an essentially expressionistic technique that is perhaps nowhere employed more successfully than in Molly Bloom's soliloquy.

Anderson's influence can be felt throughout "Poem, Story, Novel," but the piece owes much to Whitman as well. In an essay written many years later Saroyan argued that American literature began with Whitman, not Emerson.[38] Emerson was too cultivated or learned, in any case too formally educated, to be the first major American writer—the person, that is, who just began talking, ignoring whatever had been done before. Emerson's poetry was formally restrained—metricized, rhymed, and shaped in traditional patterns. Whitman showed writers how to break that restraint, forging a personal voice from a vast array of materials.[39]

Saroyan believed American writers—at least the great ones—were anarchists virtually by nature. They were willing to take risks, to be seen as lunatics if it came to that. No great moral, historical, or aesthetic motivation lay behind their work; they wrote simply "to keep up with life and to run ahead of it" (*I Used to Believe*, 137). And there was no mystery about how that was done: as Saroyan said in "Poem, Story, Novel," the writer should learn "to stand well, to breathe well, to walk well, to sleep well, to look well, to be well, and to pray piously. There are no rules other than these, and these are not rules" (*Inhale*, 288). Writing should be as unpremeditated as walking.

Like Whitman, Saroyan in part learned how to write by walking through the city listening to people talk (*After Thirty Years*, 106–7). Though Whitman sometimes used in his poems words he heard on the street, it was more than vocabulary he listened for, and the same is true for Saroyan. A sense of what Saroyan (and Whitman) found is suggested by "The Symphony," which deals with a change in the sound and tempo of American life around the time of the First World War. When Saroyan was a boy there seemed to be a kind of musical order to things that was "symphonic." It could be heard in the streets and "in patterns and rhythms of our own breathing and our own consciousness." But then "a kind of nervous noise" entered, and the rhythms of the city and everyone in it changed, and "we could almost feel it in the new way people had of doing things, of getting up and being awake, of talking, walking, of eating and working" (*Inhale*, 154–55). Such rhythms and sounds underlie Saroyan's work, and each story is in a sense a musical pattern.

But Saroyan gained more from Whitman than ideas about language. The "self" in Whitman's *Song of Myself* is not the private person. The voice is collective, and it is in Saroyan's work too. The self in Whitman's poetry spoke for, in some sense was, the voice of democracy: "every atom belonging to me as good belongs to you." Correspondingly, Saroyan believed that his voice was specifically Armenian, that it spoke for Armenia.

But in what sense could Saroyan, who did not see Armenia until he was almost 30, be considered Armenian? Zareh Yaldizdjiyan, the principal Armenian poet of this century, has argued that because Saroyan wrote in English he should be considered an American, not an Armenian, writer.[40]

Margaret Bedrosian's "William Saroyan and the Family Matter" is among the few serious critical attempts to come to terms with Saroyan as an Armenian; however, it profoundly misreads the work. She begins by saying that, like his father, Saroyan failed to write in a way that was, in his own words, "tough enough for the truth of us, of this world." For Bedrosian, the successful Armenian writers seem to be Emmanuel Varandyan, Peter Najarian, and Karl Kalfaian, who "[probe their] characters' psyches and [demonstrate] the dynamic interaction between ethnic self-awareness and other facets of human identity."[41] What she apparently wants is something within the traditions of realistic or naturalistic fiction—perhaps an Armenian version of Anzia Yezierska's powerful novel of New York's Lower East Side, *Bread Givers*. But to expect that from Saroyan would be as misguided as expecting, say, an abstract expressionist like Clyfford Still or Jackson Pollock to do figurative work.

A more profitable approach to Saroyan's sense of himself as an Armenian may lie in comparing his stories to the gestural paintings of the Armenian-American painter Arshile Gorky. The tendencies toward abstraction and expressionism in both the writer and the painter may indicate a shared politics and ethnic identity deeper than Bedrosian's approach can reach.

Gorky's paintings were originally figurative and modeled on Picasso's. Similarly, Saroyan in *Trapeze over the Universe* turned to a great modernist, Joyce. Indeed, as noted earlier, Saroyan could easily have taken as his own, Stephen Dedalus's determination at the end of *A Portrait of the Artist as a Young Man* "to forge in the smithy of my soul the uncreated conscience of my race."[42]

As they developed their respective arts, however, Gorky and, at least initially, Saroyan moved increasingly toward pure abstraction. Gorky eventually concluded that whenever the artist "stretches canvas he is drawing a new space,"[43] while Saroyan rejected mere imitation or mimesis in his fiction. For him too the work had to offer "a new space," the reason for which may have as much to do with politics as with aesthetics.

Saroyan's family had fled Armenia after the persecutions under Sultan Abdul Hamid, but they escaped the worst atrocities. Gorky and his mother, however, were among those driven into the Syrian desert in 1915, and she had died in his arms. As Armenians, both Saroyan and Gorky were without a homeland: Armenia literally did not exist except in the imagination and the shared memories of the diaspora. In turn, both found in their respective arts "a new space" that did not depend on mimesis or representation—a new space of words or colors apart from a "real" world to which writer and artist did not completely belong.

Gorky's art was more consistently and radically abstract than Saroyan's, and in what may be Gorky's greatest works he tried to realize in pure abstract forms his memories of his father's farm in Armenia. Whatever Armenia had been, it could no longer be represented; it had to be re-created, and that in effect was the impulse behind his art. A similar impulse can be felt in *Inhale and Exhale*.

The most conventional story in the section of *Inhale and Exhale* entitled "Poem, Story, Novel" is "Antranik of Armenia." The famous Armenian general seems at first a man without a country. But he is a great, not a pathetic, figure, and Saroyan's point is that although Armenia does not exist on maps or in the League of Nations, it is there in Antranik's presence and his relationships with other "countrymen." "Armenia" is an abstraction, like Gorky's paintings of his father's farm.

At this point Saroyan's aesthetics and his Armenian identity converge. "Armenia" is not there geographically or politically, yet it is still there to be expressed in the friendship of Armenians for one another and in the words of an Armenian writer. Its origin is in the self, not the world, its institutions, and its laws.

Inhale and Exhale is dedicated "[t]o the English tongue, the American earth, and the Armenian spirit" (*Inhale*, dedication page). The first gave Saroyan the words for his art; the second gave him the opportunity to speak, the opportunity that had been denied his father; but the Armenian spirit was the origin and essence of his work.

The last section of the book, "The Little Dog Laughed to See Such Sport," includes a series of journalistic sketches based on Saroyan's journey to the Soviet Union and particularly Soviet Armenia in 1935. The final sketch and, significantly, the piece with which the book ends is "The Armenian & the Armenian." In the city of Rostov, Saroyan says, the waiter at one of the restaurants he visited was Armenian. They immediately recognized each other as countrymen, began to speak their common language, and found in each other gestures and feelings that Armenians everywhere would share. The waiter was originally from Moush, a city Saroyan's father had visited when he was young. But it has now been 20 years since the Armenians were driven from that part of the world, and there were no Armenians left in that city. Everything had been done, it seemed, to destroy Armenia, but, Saroyan wrote, "See if the race will not live again when two [Armenians] meet in a beer parlor, twenty years after, and laugh, and speak in their tongue."[44]

Saroyan and the Avant-Garde

Three Times Three grew out of Saroyan's friendship with three young men from the University of Southern California who wanted to establish a new publishing firm. The Conference Press, as it was called, lasted long enough to publish just one book, Saroyan's third collection of stories. The book contains some of Saroyan's most interesting work, including "The Man with the Heart in the Highlands," "The Living and the Dead," and "Quarter, Half, Three-Quarter, and Whole Notes." The first of these was developed into his first play successfully produced on Broadway, *My Heart's in the Highlands* (1939). "The Living and the Dead" is a powerful statement of his politics, and "Quarter, Half, Three-Quarter, and Whole Notes" is his most important contribution to "the Revolution of the Word," the avant-garde aesthetic of his time.[45]

Saroyan wrote "The Man with the Heart in the Highlands" in part because he was angry over not having enough money to live as he wanted. The story is a fantasy about a world in which poets, actors, musicians, and singers can do as they want and not have to worry about dollars; the characters live in a gentle, whimsical, Saroyanesque world. They are the kind of charming eccentrics found in Saroyan's most popular works, *My Name Is Aram*, *The Time of Your Life*, and *The Human Comedy*. The narrator is a boy named Johnny, who has to fast-talk the local grocer, Mr. Kosak, into giving him food "on credit." He lives with his father, a poet who can't sell his poems, and his grandmother, who sings Puccini arias as she does her housework. A former actor, Jasper MacGregor, stops by to visit, likes what he finds, and stays 17 days. When the food runs out, he plays his bugle for the neighbors, and, in gratitude, they bring the family cheese, bread, sausage, and anything else he requests. Everyone is satisfied except Mr. Kosak, who works all the time and lectures Johnny on the importance of a steady, responsible job.

Eventually Jasper leaves in order to play the lead in the Old People's Follies of 1914, and Johnny again has to fast-talk the grocer into giving him credit. All he's able to get this time, however, is birdseed and maple syrup. The story ends the next morning with his grandmother singing like a bird.

Saroyan wanted his readers to believe his attitude toward life and career was as carefree as Jasper's. According to the preface to *Three Times Three*, it did not matter at all who published his book or who, if anyone, read it. In fact he wrote only to please himself and avoid boredom. No one should have to work, for life was a game, and writing was a good way of laughing at those who didn't think so. What Saroyan said and what he did were not always the same, however. Shortly after he finished the story, he began working as a scriptwriter for B. P. Schulberg and Columbia Studios. He was often in debt, and there were bills to pay.

"The Man with the Heart in the Highlands" was, however, a fantasy appropriate to its time. The country was in the midst of the depression. As much as a quarter of the work force couldn't find jobs. Movie-making was one of the few industries that were not financially troubled, and although Saroyan wrote the story before he went to Hollywood, clearly he already knew what had made the industry successful. In its unyielding optimism and gentle humor, "The Man with the Heart in the Highlands" is similar to the comedies of Frank Capra. The movies taught Saroyan how to create gently comic worlds in which real suffering never exists.

Saroyan's story implies that economic solutions solve very little—a point of view that certainly would have distressed writers on the Left. Although at the beginning of his career Saroyan claimed he sympathized with the Left, he eventually rejected its politics, and in "The Living and the Dead" he gave his reasons.

The Left in the 1930s was considerably fragmented, and literary critics in the radical journals were as likely to war with one another as with critics on the Right. A general rejection of modernism was evident, however, in journals as otherwise different as *Partisan Review* and the *New Masses*, and the reasons are easy to find. Whatever their differences, the leftists were bound together by a Marxist view of history that modernists generally did not share. Politics among modernist writers ranged from libertarianism (essentially Saroyan's position) to the fascism of Wyndham Lewis and Ezra Pound, but the intent in every case was to give ultimate authority to the imagination of the writer, to see him or her as a free agent, not subordinate to economics and history and certainly not subordinate to a party line. Since the whole thrust of Saroyan's work is against any kind of social or political restraint, it is odd that he ever considered himself sympathetic to the Left, yet he did, and for a while he was accepted as a fellow traveler.[46]

One wonders, however, how closely some leftist editors and critics read Saroyan's books. The *New Masses*, for example, would certainly have had no patience with the aesthetics expressed in "Poem, Story, Novel." As Malcolm Cowley wrote, the dogma at that magazine was "[d]own with technique and hurrah for writing that follows the party line."[47] Nonetheless, the *New Masses* treated Saroyan rather sympathetically, even printing his letter to the editors in which he wrote that most Communists were simply "opportunists," taking advantage of the party's popularity. Although he said, "The Communist program [was] for the most part the most valid and decent," he also believed Communism was "the style of the moment." He added that his writing would follow its own agenda (and by implication, not the party line): "it is the only writing I am able to do or give a damn about doing."[48]

Under the circumstances, the editors' response was surprisingly civil, but it was also patronizing: "Mr. Saroyan comes from the working class. Nothing has been made easy for him; he has had to fight for the right to eat and the right to dream, as have all proletarians. It is obvious that he has felt the humiliations capitalist society places on all the young proletarians of talent." Saroyan, the editors hoped, would soon come around to a correct view of things and "learn . . . the serene wisdom of Lenin and Maxim Gorky."[49]

This exchange occurred shortly after *The Daring Young Man* was published. When *Inhale and Exhale* appeared a year and a half later, it was clear that Saroyan had not done his political homework. Christina Stead, reviewing the new book for the *New Masses*, concluded that "Saroyan knows so little and gives himself so little to think about that his attention has become fixed on bodily functions like a convalescent; and he is excited by inhaling and exhaling." Nonetheless, she was willing to grant that "this king of kaffee-klatsch" did possess a sort of "genius" that could be found when he "scribbles along gaily, madly about the things he knows best, the foreign-born population of America and the pool parlors, barber shops, hobo young men."[50] In other words, Saroyan was a proletarian writer not yet in control of his craft. In saying this, however, Stead missed the point, complimenting him for subject matter that to his way of thinking could not be separated from his method.

Three Times Three gave Saroyan the opportunity to respond to critics like Stead. In his introductory note to "Public Speech" he wrote that he admired "the Communists for being able to be stupid enough to believe there is hope for collective man." Given the kinds of stupidity in the world, at least for the present this was "a very desirable variety of it." Neither Communists nor the masses were "spiritually equipped to face the inward tragedy which occurs with genuine knowing."[51] This point of view is found also in "The Living and the Dead," which Edmund Wilson, in spite of his own leanings to the Left, considered "one of the best things Saroyan has written."[52]

"The Living and the Dead" contrasts the utopian visions of the Communists with the memories of the narrator's Armenian grandmother, who believes that bitterness and hatred will never be exorcised from the world. Based on Saroyan's own grandmother, she is one of the most powerful figures in his stories. Her suffering has given her an emotional intensity and insight into the nature of people that makes social reformers seem shallow and unrealistic.

"Which tribe of the earth was kind to our tribe?" she asks her grandson (*Three*, 43). People treated his grandfather well only because they were afraid of him. She has fled to America from a world of bitter hatreds. The Armenian language, she says, "is a tongue of bitterness. We have tasted much of death and our tongue is heavy with hatred and anger" (*Three*, 46). She has no use for reformers who think happiness will come when everyone has enough money. The problem is "poverty of spirit. . . . Give them all the money in the world and they'll still be poor" (*Three*, 50).

Her husband, she says, was the only man who could speak Armenian "as if it were the tongue of a God-like people." Somehow he had discovered a way to live in spite of the pain, but "if he was drunk, . . . you'd think God in Heaven was crying lamentations and oaths upon the tribes of the earth" (*Three*, 46). Although the narrator at first rejects his grandmother's point of view, subsequent events convince him that she sees the world as it is, and he begins to understand everything as entangled in a "heritage of errors" (*Three*, 52).

Wilson thought that the story, good as it was, ultimately failed because it did not resolve the issues it raised (Wilson, 30). But in fact Saroyan's decision is clear. The world seems "an absurdity, an insanity," and the reformers have no solutions (*Three*, 53). Whether or not they are sincere, their utopian program is not enough to resolve the suffering in the world. Simply changing the social structure would only change the rules, not eliminate misery itself. Given the world as it is, the writer "admire[s] most those men of wisdom who accept the tragic obligation to be irresponsible until the time when sincerity will have become natural and noble and not artificial and vicious as it is now" (*Three*, 53–54).

Saroyan's politics are exactly what one should expect from a writer who refused any rules, any conventions in his own work. Had he been no more than a popular writer, critics on the Left could simply have dismissed him. But he was also widely seen as a serious writer, and sooner or later he would have to be answered. Among those on the Left, no one formulated the case against Saroyan better than Philip Rahv in an article for *Partisan Review*, a journal he edited with William Phillips.

In the early 1930s William Phillips, who founded *Partisan Review* with Rahv in 1934, set out to write, within a Marxist framework, a book that would admit the modernists' political shortcomings while admiring their literary achievements; however, the paradox was too deep to resolve, and he eventually abandoned the work.[53] Since modernist politics and aesthetics were seemingly inseparable, the only solution lay in an avant-garde that would reject not only the politics but also the theories about writing, and Phillips thought he found in the new generation the writers he was looking for. As he wrote in his autobiography many years later, "One has only to think of magazines like *Transition*, *Broom*, *Pagany*, and of the surrealist and dadaists, to realize that their irrationality, eccentricity, dedication to language and experiment and commitment to spontaneity had been supplanted by a broader, more sober perspective that attempted to reconcile the tradition of modernism with a sense of history, with an awareness of the entire culture, and with a feeling for the bizarre quality of individual lives. Obviously, anything like a celebration of the 'revolution of the word' . . . would seem outdated in such an intellectual atmosphere."[54] To Phillips and Rahv, history was Marxist and progressive—a position in every way opposite to Saroyan's darker, fatalistic position.

Rahv's review of *The Daring Young Man* in the summer of 1935 argued that Saroyan "illustrates a literary trend or symptom of social importance." Rahv believed writing was shaped by "world-feeling"—in other words, language was secondary to history and politics. But Saroyan, he argued, was terrified by "objective life" and had retreated to "the seductive mystery of the dream of stasis." For Saroyan, language was material out of which the writer built a fortress against the threatening world, and in doing so he had aligned himself with "the school of esthetes-modernists." "Here at last," Rahv concluded, "is the mystery of Pound and Jolas and Cummings and Williams wriggling on the ground, in full view," yet they had done it "when the mode had a stronger base because of the absence, in the cultural sphere at least, of its dialectic opponent and conqueror."[55] Rahv, by formulating his argument in this way, was able to excuse the great modernists for their shortcomings (the necessary political corrective hadn't yet emerged) while dismissing Saroyan as an anachronism, an echo of certain unfortunate political tendencies among his literary mentors.

Although Rahv's criticism became less stridently Marxist with the passage of time, he continued to see literature as secondary to history. He became a spokesman for those who valued intellect and reflection over "the cult of experience," as he called it.[56] Modernists like Yeats, Pound, and Lawrence assumed a "sovereignty of the word, not only in literature but also in life," while for Rahv, as for his own mentor, Trotsky, "in the beginning was the deed, with the word following as its 'phonetic shadow.'"[57] Given that position, there was no ground on which Saroyan and Rahv could meet. Their assumptions about the origins and use of language could hardly have been further apart.

Rahv was in any case correct in seeing Saroyan as a latter-day modernist. Sherwood Anderson had begun publishing a generation before Saroyan, and although *Winesburg, Ohio* had once seemed innovative and experimental, by the 1930s he too was under attack from the new avant-garde. The revolution of which Anderson was a part was not over, however, and throughout the decade writers as different as Henry Miller, William Faulkner, Anaïs Nin, Thomas Wolfe, and William Everson continued to do major work in an expressionist tradition ultimately rooted in Whitman. In the end, the political Left faded with the economic crisis that had called it into being, and by the 1950s, many of the writers the Left admired, particularly proletarian novelists and Marxist poets, were passé while Saroyan, Miller, and Anderson were imitated and read by a new generation of writers.

The most radical instance of Saroyan's aesthetics in *Three Times Three* is "Quarter, Half, Three-Quarter, and Whole Notes." In the first and last paragraphs Saroyan restates his belief that stories do not begin with consideration of such technical matters as plot and style: these must arise naturally from the writing itself. Form is derived from an order, or "wholeness," the writer finds within the self. "A story (or any other work of art)," he said, "does not occur when one does the actual writing: it began to occur when one began to live consciously and piously" (*Three*, 137). "A narrative in order to be a narrative," Saroyan added, "need no longer concern itself solely with physical events in the lives of men (this is history); on the contrary, it should concern itself with the subtlest and most evanescent of universal meanings evolving from all the facts which make for consciousness in man" (*Three*, 159).

Saroyan sounds as if he were arguing for lyric poetry rather than prose fiction, and "Quarter, Half, Three-Quarter, and Whole Notes" is largely a series of lyrical notations with little apparent relation to one another except that they collectively illustrate what Saroyan meant by narrative. The story is in effect a set of interrelated prose poems or notations, some of them surrealistic, others sentimental, exuberant, or merely silly:

If you laugh loudly, you are bound to weep bitterly. Walk in the valley, and through the dark city walk. See. (*Three*, 157)

In 1926 they were singing Valencia, in my dreams. Do you remember the cigarettes? And traffic turning the corner? (*Three*, 158)

Irish songs: Oh, didn't you hear the glorious news that happened at Ballyhooly? Dan Tutty the gauger was caught and thrashed by Paddy and Timothy Dooly. (*Three*, 158)

Saroyan's stories, as we have seen, frequently depend on lyrical modulations of this sort, but here lyricism is the work itself. There is no conventional narrative or characterization, yet in Saroyan's terms what is left is still a "story." "Plot, atmosphere, style, and all the rest of it," he said, "may be regarded as so much nonsense: it is impossible to write one paragraph about man without having plot, and atmosphere, and what is known as style" (*Three*, 160).[58]

In 1936 that position would have been no more widely understood or appreciated than it is now, and to publish his more innovative works Saroyan needed either a small press (such as the one that published *Three Times Three*) or a sympathetic editor at one of the little magazines. Most of his short fiction in the 1930s consequently appeared in little magazines like *Twice a Year*, *transition*, and *New Directions*, as well as in lesser-known periodicals like *Direction*, *Genesis*, and *Tramp*. In 1946 the authors of *The Little Magazine* claimed that Saroyan's "interest in little magazines has been unceasing and healthful."[59] They pointed out that one magazine, the *Dubuque Dial* (1934–35), had made its reputation by favoring stories in the Saroyan manner, while another, *Horizon* (1936–37), sold itself largely on the basis of his contributions.

These magazines were enormously important to Saroyan, for if they paid their contributors little or nothing, at least there was no pressure to conform to a popular market or to a restricting editorial policy such as that at the *New Masses* or *Partisan Review*. Basically the little magazines allowed Saroyan to write as he wished, and his vast productivity in the late 1930s may have had much to do with the fact that he could always find publishers, even for his most extreme statements and experiments.

One of the magazines to which Saroyan contributed was Robert Lowry's *Little Man*, founded in 1938 when the editor was an undergraduate at the University of Cincinnati. A year later Lowry published the second issue (priced at 8¢ a copy), containing a story and a series of fragments by Saroyan. Saroyan also contributed an essay on "American Qualities" to J. Calder Joseph's *Narration with a Red Piano*, a book of poems the Little Man Press issued a year later. The essay offered typical Saroyan advice for young writers. Concern with the traditional elements of fiction was all wrong, he said: "Don't let form (the mechanics: technique and so on) hinder anybody. If a man says twenty words that are fresh and genuine, these words *are themselves form*."[60]

Although it is likely Saroyan reached few readers through Lowry's publications, everything Lowry did was well designed and well printed. More important, Saroyan had the satisfaction of knowing he was being read by a new generation of serious young writers. In this way little magazines could sustain his identity as a serious writer, one who was in a position to influence others, as he had been influenced by Anderson. And the little magazines were also a reminder that Philip Rahv and *Partisan Review* did not represent the only avant-garde.

One important little magazine for which Saroyan wrote was *Story*, which reached precisely the audience most concerned with short fiction as an art; however, the editors chose the contents of their magazine from a variety of traditions, not just Saroyan's. On the other hand, the various *Hairenik* publications, directed at the Armenian-American community, gave him an audience of great personal value but one perhaps less interested in his aesthetic intentions.[61]

One of the most significant little magazines with which Saroyan was associated was *transition*. Perhaps the most self-consciously avant-garde of all little magazines at the time, *transition* was dedicated to an ideal of pure poetry, which the editor, Eugene Jolas, defined as "A LYRICAL ABSOLUTE THAT SEEKS AN A PRIORI REALITY WITHIN OURSELVES ALONE."[62] *transition*'s motto was "the Revolution of the Word," and its principal contributors included Stein, Joyce, Laura Riding, Louis Zukofsky, and Samuel Beckett. The magazine is generally considered one of the principal means through which surrealism reached English readers, but as Donald McMillan pointed out in his history of *transition*, Jolas was also interested in expressionism; hence expressionist writers were frequently published in his magazine.[63]

Jolas maintained that "the literature of the future will tend . . . towards the poet's exploration of heretofore hidden strata of the human personality." He believed traditional genres would be abandoned. Specifically, in place of "the short story or *nouvelle*" he thought there would be what he called "the paramyth," seen as "a kind of epic wonder tale giving an organic synthesis of the individual and universal consciousness—the dream, daydream, the mystic vision" (Jolas, 29). This description at least approximates what Saroyan was doing in some of his more fanciful works, such as "The Man with His Heart in the Highlands," a fusion of expressionist and surrealist aesthetics.

But if Saroyan was indebted to Jolas he also had reservations about some of the more extreme manifestations of the Revolution of the Word.

Saroyan contributed two pieces to *transition*, and both were published in 1938 in the magazine's final issue. The more interesting of the two, simply called "Fragment," is a parody of the fragments of Joyce's work in progress (not yet called *Finnegans Wake*), which Jolas had been publishing for several years and for which *transition* was famous. To some readers these fragments must have seemed little more than exercises in multilingual incoherence, and Saroyan's parody is a series of apparent non sequiturs, beginning with "In my room I slept, dreaming language" and followed by a jumble of words from Dutch, Italian, French, and various other languages ("Sea hecha tua volontad come all ye faithful como en el cielo, friend, can you tell me the way to Troy?" and so on), ending with an address to a woman in which the narrator says he has brought her his "money on a copy of True Confessions."[64] Could Jolas possibly have considered this a serious contribution to his "Revolution of the Word"? And if he didn't, why did he publish a work that could very well have offended his most famous contributor? Although Saroyan had great respect for *Ulysses*, he evidently had other feelings about the work in progress.

"The Slot Machine (Extracts)," Saroyan's other contribution to *tradition*, was an even stranger work for Jolas to publish. Saroyan seems to have exuberantly typed whatever came to mind, all of it having something to do with a Mr. Fleming and "big broad Texas, big Texas broad, lone star Trixie."[65] The story also sounds like some of the more garbled and pretentious experiments Jolas published, and its conclusion may be Saroyan's farewell to "innovative" writers whose only contributions to the Revolution of the Word were new degrees of incoherence: "Train going. Farewell you cockeyed palookas. Going. Farewell you highly educated brats and bores. Going. Farewell you wealthy baboons. Farewell you jitney philosophers. Going. Farewell you polite thieves" (*Three*, 130).

Of all the little magazines in which Saroyan published his stories, none better represented his ideas on fiction and gave him a more appreciative audience than Henry Miller's *Booster*. Miller advocated essentially the same expressionist program as Saroyan. The formalist traditions, sacred to the *Partisan* and *Kenyon* reviews, bored him: "I dislike Henry James intensely, and absolutely detest Edgar Allan Poe." He claimed that the only American writers who had influenced him were Emerson and Whitman and that the only genre in which American literature was really good was the short story, the masters of which ("the equals of . . . any European, in this realm") included Anderson and Saroyan.[66] For Miller as for Saroyan, the boundary between fiction and autobiography (or any other genre) was never precise: his novel *Tropic of Cancer* was "an autobiographical document, a *human* book" (Miller, 161).

Like Saroyan, Miller greatly disliked abstract thought and trusted only the direct expression of the self. "I believe only in what is active, immediate and personal," he wrote (Miller, 160). Ideas for him were inseparable from the person who spoke them, and his most important predecessor (as important for him as Anderson was for Saroyan) and the subject of one of his earliest critical studies was D. H. Lawrence. Lawrence's "quality," Miller said, "has nothing to do with the question of right or wrong. What endears him to me is his ability to express himself as completely as he did."[67]

Miller's expressionism, like the expressive quality he found in Lawrence, was rooted in sexuality, whereas Saroyan's expressionism derived from ethnic identity. Miller and Saroyan were in fact very different from each other, but at first they saw only what they had in common. Eventually they stopped writing or speaking to each other. (Miller concluded that although Saroyan was "today the most daring of all our storytellers," he was "timid," and that although he had taken "a big hurdle in the beginning, . . . he refuses to go on hurdling.")[68] In the late 1930s, however, their shared expressionist aesthetics bound them together in opposition to a literary and critical world preoccupied with a writer's politics.

Shortly after *The Daring Young Man* was published Miller wrote to Saroyan from Paris, welcoming him as "the only real writer in the United States,"[69] and Saroyan responded by calling Miller "one of the great ones."[70] Both were friendly with Hilaire Hiler and contributed essays to his book on expressionist theory, *Why Abstract?*, and together they helped make the *Booster* one of the decade's most exotic and genuinely revolutionary literary magazines.

The *Booster* was originally the official and staid publication of the American Country Club in Paris. The club's president, surely not knowing quite what he was doing, hired Miller's friend Alfred Perlès in 1937 as the editor. Perlès in turn appointed Saroyan, Miller, and Lawrence Durrell as literary editors, Anaïs Nin as "society editor," and Walter Lowenfels (who came from a family that had made its fortune in butter) as "butter editor." The new policy was that the magazine would have no policy.

The editors published three issues before the country club and the advertisers withdrew their support. In the meantime, however, "The Man with the Heart in the Highlands" and "Poem, Story, Novel" were printed, and Miller and his friends, most of whom were expressionist writers, created the movement's most famous little magazine in English. There was a fourth, much shorter issue, whereupon the *Booster* was retitled the *Delta*, but after three more issues it ceased publication in early 1939. Saroyan and the other *Booster* writers found another little magazine, *Seven*, that was sympathetic to their work, and until that magazine in turn folded in 1940, at the outbreak of the war, it served as an outlet for their work.

With the beginning of the war, the first great period of little magazines came to an end. Paper was in short supply, and many of the editors and writers were in the armed forces. Saroyan published nine collections of short stories between 1934 and 1941 but only one more until *The Assyrian* appeared in 1950. By the time a second great wave of little magazines came along after the war, he was established primarily as a popular novelist and playwright, with an audience very different from the avant-garde he had cultivated in the days of the *Booster,* the *Little Man,* and the Conference Press.

Versions of Solitude

In 1938, when the first wave of Saroyan's popularity had passed, he published an autobiographical sketch titled simply "Saroyan" in which he made the rather extraordinary (but altogether serious) claim that he was naturally "great."[71] He didn't explain how or why; apparently he felt that should be obvious to his readers.

Saroyan's "monumental self-esteem," his biographers wrote, "was . . . the very heart of his public image, like Jack Benny's stinginess or W. C. Fields's fondness for the bottle."[72] Surely Saroyan's arrogance and assurance were in part an act that got his name into newspapers and helped sell books, but he also needed considerable self-confidence to continue writing as he did while ignoring his critics.

By 1936 or 1937 he had plainly lost much of his early popularity. Neither his second book nor his third sold as well as the first. In *Three Times Three* he claimed that popularity was not what he was looking for, but his next four collections of short fiction were made up exclusively of stories that were accessible, easily read, and rarely "experimental." They had little to do with avant-garde aesthetics and the Revolution of the Word.

Many of the stories in the first (and best) of these collections, *Little Children* (1937), are drawn from Saroyan's childhood in Fresno. Like Sherwood Anderson's *Winesburg, Ohio*, the book is a set of stories closely linked in tone and theme. Although not equal to Saroyan's earlier books, it is much better than its relative neglect would indicate: although Saroyan scholars and critics seldom mention it and it has long been out of print, it was Saroyan's first book to be fashioned according to the pattern he used in *The Human Comedy* and *My Name Is Aram*, and it contains some interesting work.

The "children" in many of the stories are first- or second-generation immigrants who have never been able to take full control of their lives. Their enemies are "Americans"—people, that is, whose only distinction is that their ancestors arrived earlier yet who now have the money and power to make the world do what they want. "Everything I write, everything I have ever written," Saroyan said, "is allegorical,"[73] and in a sense his Americans are really Ottomans in disguise, while his "children" are the Armenians, Kurds, Arabs, Greeks, and Turks who suffered under them. But his dislike of Americans was real if not always well formulated. An American, he wrote near the beginning of *Little Children*, was "an incompetent who [despises] people of other races because they [aren't] incompetent."[74] Here and in other books his Americans tend to be teachers, businessmen, and officials who want to make immigrants useful, productive, and obedient. Immigrants, on the other hand, have traditions and values that a successful if "incompetent" American could not understand.

The first story in *Little Children* is "The Man Who Got Fat." The narrator is a 14-year-old messenger boy who works for Nathan Katz, "said to be the world's fastest telegraph operator." Katz, who is Jewish, works in turn for Americans who live in a part of the city "where an Armenian couldn't buy a house even if he had the money" (*Little*, 111–12). Sending and receiving their telegrams, he learns how they made their fortunes and decides to see whether he too can do that. He succeeds, but none of the Americans will accept him as one of their own, and in the meantime he has cut himself off from his own people and heritage. Saroyan's obvious point is that even if one imitates those in charge, it is impossible ever to be accepted by them. "The Man Who Got Fat" reverses the myth of America as a land of opportunity. Whatever "opportunities" America offers the immigrant are ambiguous, taking more than they give.

The narrator of "Many Miles per Hour" says that as a boy his hero was "Speed" Wallace, a rich young man who drove fast cars through the city and whose great ambition was to win races at the local track. Winning was all that mattered. On the other hand, in "Where I Come from People Are Polite" a young man quits his job and steals a motorcycle to ride it along a beach. The difference between him and Americans like Speed Wallace is that the Americans merely want success, while Saroyan's hero is in search of a special moment of freedom.

Sarkis Khatchadourian in "Countryman, How Do You Like America," feels terribly alone in America but is sustained by his Armenian identity and his memory of his lost homeland. He has no great need to succeed; his sense of himself as an Armenian is all he needs to survive in his solitude. The Jewish boy in "Laughing Sam" can get only menial jobs, but he carries within himself an ancient past and is justified by it: "He wept from the beginning of his life, ten centuries ago" (*Little*, 12). The immigrant is usually poor but sustained by his traditions and community, whereas the Americans are left only with their ambitions.

"Around the World with General Grant," however, suggests there are threats against which even one's community and traditions offer no protection. In this story a young boy forgets to get off the train at his stop and, alone in the dark, has to find his way home from the next town. As he does so he becomes aware of a disorder within himself—an "unholy presence" that could rise up and destroy "the century after century of mortality in [himself]" (*Little*, 129).

There is terrifying ambiguity in the solitude many of Saroyan's heroes choose—a solitude that frees them from an oppressive or indifferent world but leaves them vulnerable, like the boy in the night, to an inner, destructive, "unholy presence." Saroyan's fiction characteristically avoids pointing to conclusions so darkly explicit, but they can frequently be felt around the edges of the fiction. The daring young man, after all, chooses a route that frees him from the world but is at the same time self-destructive. That, however, is a conclusion the reader draws—it is not something Saroyan says. "Around the World with General Grant" is unusual among Saroyan's works, one of the few stories in which he was willing to suggest directly that an individual could be threatened as much by forces within himself as by the world.

Aram Saroyan wrote that his father was "essentially an *entertainer*," regularly displaying "his stock of tried and true effects, his own perennial bag of tricks"[75]—a description that, however arguable it may be in reference to the best of Saroyan's early work, does fit what he was doing in his stories during the late 1930s and early 1940s. Those stories are generally slick and predictable, and there is nothing among them as interesting as "The Living and the Dead" or "Seventy Thousand Assyrians."

However "Saroyanesque" the early work may be, it has its darkness and threats—the Assyrian's knowledge that his family and race will disappear, the Armenian's belief that her language is a language of bitterness. The stories published in the latter half of the 1930s are rarely so dark as this. Instead there is a pervasive melancholy like that in Saroyan's most famous play, *The Time of Your Life* (1939). These stories are about people who drink to ease their sadness, to help them forget the girl who left, the friendship that didn't work out, the dreams of success that will never be realized. Very little actually happens in these stories; essentially they are generalized complaints.

For example, Joe Silvera in "The Trains," one of the better pieces in *Love, Here Is My Hat,* is an artist who has had no commercial success. To him the trains departing from the station near his apartment seem melancholy and sad. He feels homeless, rootless, and thinks about taking a train somewhere, anywhere, if only to escape the horrible lethargy and despair he feels settling in himself. A morning in a local bar leaves him feeling warm and friendly, however, and he drifts over to a park nearby and falls asleep under a tree. When he wakes up, he sees a girl sitting near him. She seems friendly, and he decides to ask her to go back to his rooms with him and to let her choose whether he should go through with his plan to escape from his world. She spends the night with him; however, the next day when he tries to interest her in his painting she is indifferent, and the sound of the trains does not have the special meaning for her that it has for him. As soon as he can, he gets her to leave the apartment and begins to pack his paintings in preparation for the morning train.

There is no potential for tragedy in stories like this, for people like Silvera are essentially victims, seldom responsible for their fate. They have been dealt a bad hand and are caught in a world that has little use for them. Nor does anyone suffer deeply; the controlling emotion is melancholy. There is no great tension in these stories either. Aside from their characteristic poignancy and melancholy, they tend to be bland and arid—altogether different from the intensity and energy of *Inhale and Exhale.* This kind of story certainly has its advocates, however, and has been widely imitated. Raymond Carver was among its successful practitioners.

These stories are important as a record of America after the initial glitter and excitement of city life had vanished and people found themselves without real communities, each person so fully alone that individualism had become merely the condition of things and not an Emersonian ideal. Charlie Chaplin had transformed that condition into pathos and comedy, and Saroyan at times tried to achieve the same effect in his fiction, notably in various episodes in *The Human Comedy.* The situations in some stories are in fact so similar to those in Chaplin's *City Lights* (1931) and *Modern Times* (1936) that an influence seems likely, but Chaplin was able to imply a complexity and resilience in the persona he created that Saroyan never matched in his stories. Yet Saroyan's drifters and loners do help define a national malaise, an emotional geography that Emersonian self-reliance never took into account.

* * *

Arrogance reached new heights in Saroyan's dedication to *The Trouble with Tigers* (1938). This was a book, he said, for "the bad writer who is grateful for good writing" and "the good writer who knows that good contemporaries make him better."[76] And he was entirely serious.

In the principal story, "The Tiger," a young man named John Brooke (who has not yet actually written anything) is said to be more of a writer than those he meets (an author of detective stories, a specialist in romantic fiction, and a political propagandist) because everything he does amounts to the one book of his life. To be a writer has to do with living, not words. It is a way of keeping the "tigers" at bay and means always being carefree, never really being concerned about anything that threatens. Asked by the proletarian writer what he "intend[s] to do about Fascism," Brooke says he will "wait for it to end" (*Trouble*, 11). "The Tiger" is supposed to be politically serious (or at least serious in suggesting that it is a very bad thing to be serious), but in fact it is pompous.

A similar piece is "We Want a Touchdown." After claiming he was "probably one of the noisiest [writers] that ever broke into print" (a claim no one could reasonably dispute), Saroyan says he advised his cousin always when setting out to do something to make "your beginning with style": "By style I meant combining in your behavior an awareness of your talent and an attitude concerning it that was honestly certain, if not downright conceited. You've got to do that, I told him, or else they won't know the truth about you because they aren't very bright" (*Trouble*, 260).

That attitude was unlikely either to encourage good writing or to win readers, and, not surprisingly, *The Trouble with Tigers* sold poorly. The book had only two printings, and Saroyan estimated that even if one counted library patrons, it never reached more than 10,000 people—a very modest number for any of his works.[77] In 1944 it was reissued in paperback as *"Some Day I'll Be a Millionaire": 34 More Great Stories*, but it was never as widely known and reviewed as Saroyan's early books.

Saroyan's next book, *Peace, It's Wonderful* (1939), was a miscellaneous collection of stories, essays, and parodies. The parodies include "The Warm, Quiet Valley of Home," "What We Want Is Love and Money," and "The War in Spain," all of which imitate Hemingway's clipped, spare prose. "At the Chop Suey Joint on Larkin Street at Two Thirty in the Morning," "The Love Kick," and "Johnny the Dreamer, May the Model at Magnin's, and Plato the Democrat" parody Ring Lardner's first-person narratives written in vernacular American English. Saroyan's parodies, as in the opening of "Poem, Story, Novel," can be quite clever. In his Hemingway and Lardner pieces, however, he only imitated surface mannerisms; there was no special understanding of what those writers had achieved.

The book also includes a series of "Little Moral Tales"—examples of comic Middle Eastern stories that Saroyan had been publishing in Armenian magazines and would collect two years later in his *Fables*. In general these pieces deal with ways in which "little people" outwit those who have greater power and money. The tone is obviously different from that which he had cultivated in "The Trains." On the other hand, "Noonday Dark Enfolding Texas," the best work in the volume, describes one of the dust storms that swept through midwestern states during the 1930s and, in its unemotional, factual tone, unusual for Saroyan, implies resignation to an inevitable and hopeless situation. There is no pathos or melancholy.

But most of the stories are quite sentimental. "Romance," for example, concerns a young man who likes to daydream and falls in love with the girl sitting across the aisle from him on a train. They talk for a while, and eventually she moves across the aisle to sit beside him. As the story ends, he dreams about marrying her. The English poet Stevie Smith took strong exception to such stories; she felt they had "a soft centre . . . which is rather sickly," and the "solemn bits" made her "glad that the Atlantic" separated the author from her.[78]

Although *Dear Baby* was not published until 1944, it should be considered with the books of short stories Saroyan published in the late 1930s. Essentially it is a miscellaneous collection of short pieces that had been written and published as early as 1935 but had not found a place in any of his previous books. Riding the crest of the enormous popularity of *My Name Is Aram* and *The Human Comedy,* Saroyan simply swept together enough to make a new book (but barely that, for the volume contains only 117 pages of large type).

There is a great range of stories in *Dear Baby*—everything from deeply sentimental writing like that in *The Human Comedy* to experimental pieces, including a revised version of the pieces published in *transition.* The former is represented particularly by the title story, a painfully maudlin work in which a prize-fighter mourns the death of his girlfriend by playing their favorite song on a Victrola she bought. It says much about Saroyan's sense of his audience that he made this the title piece of the collection and placed it first, burying the more experimental works toward the back: *The Human Comedy* had shown him exactly where his market lay.

"Mr. Fleming and the Seven Wonders of the World" is a revision of sentences and passages originally included in "The Slot-Machine (Extracts)" and "Fragment." The audience for *Dear Baby*, however, would surely have included many who would neither know nor care about the excesses of Eugene Jolas's Revolution of the Word and Joyce's work in progress, and so the most pointed references to those things have been removed. The multiple-language nonsense is gone, along with Saroyan's good-bye to the more pretentious members of the avant-garde. Instead there are two pages of silliness—a stream of giddy, exuberant talk Saroyan always could do well: "I sat there all day, remembering the face of Leonora, chanting the devotional exercises of Christians of various denominations: nothing but love (baby): I got a woman crazy for me."[79]

Several of the stories are drawn from Saroyan's boyhood Armenian community and his sense of ethnic identity: "The Hummingbird," "The Declaration of War," "How It Is to Be," and so forth. In "The Struggle of Jim Patros with Death" a Greek waiter who everyone decides is on his deathbed instead survives; he does so, his doctor says, because before he came to America he never wore shoes, and "from the earth . . . came the strength of the old country" (*Dear Baby*, 60).

The writing in *Love, Here Is My Hat; The Trouble with Tigers; Peace, It's Wonderful;* and *Dear Baby* is characterized by slick, professional surfaces as if Saroyan knew exactly what he was doing as he did it, the effects and impressions he wanted to produce. This quality, of course, is the exact opposite of what expressionism, as he had defined it in "Poem, Story, Novel," is supposed to achieve—discovery in the act of writing itself.

Saroyan's work in the late 1930s and the 1940s can be highly calculating and altogether distinct from the kind of fiction he earlier practiced. Although he continued to advocate expressionist aesthetics,[80] his own work suggested a writer who has mastered and now cleverly manipulates a restricted field of verbal mannerisms and techniques. He was less a "writer" like John Brooke in "The Tiger" than one of the professionals the story criticizes. Indeed, by this time the Saroyan story was itself a recognized type and Saroyan in effect had become his own best imitator.

In 1940 Edmund Wilson, in "The Boys in the Backroom," his study of West Coast writers, accused Saroyan of being a Hemingway imitator (Wilson, 26). Hemingway himself had suggested the same thing in an article published in *Esquire* in 1935 shortly after *The Daring Young Man* first appeared. It would take a lot more time and practice for Saroyan to begin doing something uniquely his own, Hemingway implied, and real success would mean having a purpose—that is, doing more than just talking about himself. As far as Hemingway could see, the only thing new about Saroyan was that he was Armenian.[81]

Saroyan, however, always denied he was copying Hemingway.[82] There are obvious but superficial similarities, largely resulting from the fact that both had learned their trade from Anderson.[83] While Hemingway was the rigorous craftsman, carefully reworking his prose, Saroyan in his earliest and best stories avoided revision, thus preserving his characteristic freshness and immediacy.

In *Short Drive, Sweet Chariot* Saroyan said he had used Hemingway's "spare style" in "A Curved Line" in *The Daring Young Man* only because he was too tired to write the way he usually did. His own writing was "all over the place"—an accurate if unflattering description of much of his early prose.[84] Despite his claims, the stories published and collected in the latter part of the 1930s ("The Trains," for example) are generally written in a "spare style." The model, however, was probably not Hemingway but the movies.

For better or worse, Saroyan's work as a scenarist required a tighter, more direct prose than he had generally been using. For a while he worked as a script doctor, which meant, among other things, that he was supposed to condense and clarify matters of plot and character. Information in movies had to be conveyed as quickly as possible, especially in dialogue. Characters had to be immediately recognizable types. In place of the long, loosely woven story-essays characteristic of his first three books, Saroyan began at this time to write his short, clipped anecdotal pieces, many of them heavily dependent on dialogue.

The movies may have influenced Saroyan in another way. Whereas early works like "Seventy Thousand Assyrians" are intensely subjective, stories like "The Train" and "The Tigers" are marked by the writer keeping his distance, narrating events while remaining separate from them. In these later stories Saroyan is more like the scenarist making a film than the writer at his typewriter putting down whatever comes to mind. Although both modes can be found throughout Saroyan's career ("Noonday Dark Enfolding Texas," for example, is more like his earlier work), the work from 1934 to 1939 reflects a definite shift to a seemingly more objective stance.

Hollywood may also have taught Saroyan something about marketing. He was one of the first important American writers to seek a wider audience through mass-market paperback books. Paperbacks were in part a response to the depression and the war economy. They seemed a good way to bring back readers who could not afford conventional books (then about $2.50) and became increasingly popular in the late 1930s and early 1940s.

Love, Here Is My Hat (1938) was originally published by Modern Age in paperback at 25¢, and Saroyan thought copies "would sell like hot-cakes in the universities."[85] Things did not work out quite that way, however; nor did paperback publication make *Peace, It's Wonderful* a popular success. In part the problem was that Modern Age paperbacks were sold only in bookstores. On the other hand, Avon, which was founded in 1942 and began publishing Saroyan's work the same year, distributed its paperbacks largely through newsstands and variety stores. Avon reissued *The Trouble with Tigers* and combined *Love, Here Is My Hat* and *Peace, It's Wonderful* under the title *48 Saroyan Stories*. The following year the company published, again in paperback, *From Inhale and Exhale*, with only half the selections in the original volume. Avon paperbacks were directed at a popular market, and it says much that the publisher neither reissued *Three Times Three* nor included "Poem, Story, Novel" in its edition of *From Inhale and Exhale*.

Paperbacks, in any case, were in part responsible for Saroyan's second great wave of popularity. *My Name Is Aram* (1940), which was distributed both in a mass-market paperback edition and in a special paper edition published for the armed forces, became one of his best-known works. Paperbacks also helped define the new audience for whom his most popular work, *The Human Comedy*, was written.

Success and Defeat

Although the stories that made Saroyan famous were expressionistic, near the beginning of his career he had mastered a more objective, crafted form of storytelling derived from Middle Eastern folktales. An early example is "The Barber Whose Uncle Had His Head Bitten off by a Circus Tiger," one of the better stories collected in *Inhale and Exhale*. In this story an Armenian barber tells the narrator, an 11-year-old boy, about "poor uncle Misak," a wrestler who traveled everywhere looking for work. But he found no work, no friends, no shelter, only "this loneliness of man in the world. This tragic loneliness of the living."[86] Finally an Arab in China found him a job in a French circus, sticking his head in the mouth of a tiger. For a while everything went well, but when the circus reached Teheran the tiger suddenly turned mean. "My poor uncle Misak," said the barber, "placed his head into the yawning mouth of the tiger, in Teheran, that ugly rotting city of Persia, and he was about to take his head out of the tiger's mouth when the tiger, full of the ugliness of things living on the earth, clapped its jaws together" (*Inhale*, 169). While the barber has been telling his story, he has given the narrator a terrible haircut, but the boy doesn't care, even when everybody laughs at the way he looks. All he wants is for his hair to get long again so that he can go back to the barber "and listen to his story of man on earth, lost and lonely and always in danger. . . . The sad story of every man alive" (*Inhale*, 170).

"The Barber Whose Uncle Had His Head Bitten off by a Circus Tiger" brings together the two narrative modes Saroyan developed in *My Name Is Aram* and *Saroyan's Fables*, respectively. The stories in the first are modeled on Anderson; those in the second are drawn from Armenian folk traditions. Anderson's way of telling a story is often rambling and discursive (indeed, "The Barber Whose Uncle Had His Head Bitten off by a Circus Tiger" is nearly two-thirds complete before the story of uncle Misak and the tiger begins), but the fable is told to point out a specific moral, idea, or conclusion, and everything must be focused toward that end. Fables are formal, schematic stories, not much different in kind from crafted tales by Poe, whose fiction Saroyan disliked,[87] but in practice he could work as successfully in one mode as the other.

The Garoghlanian family in Saroyan's most important collection of short stories, *My Name Is Aram* (1940), have "been famous for . . . honesty for something like eleven centuries."[88] That is, they trace their roots, or at least their honesty, back to the ninth century, the beginning of the finest period in Armenian history, literature, and art. The Garoghlanians, in other words, were there from the start, and the narrator, Aram, is named for a legendary patriarch said to have ruled 4,000 years earlier.

But the Garoghlanians are now in America, where well-meaning people call Aram "Eugene" and his friend Panvor "Pandro." The Americans want to transform immigrants into potential "captains of industry." The Garoghlanians have other intentions: they simply want to be Armenian and to survive.

As Saroyan wrote of his own family, "when a great many of the Armenians of Bitlis saw that the future for them in Bitlis was at best only heroic, with violent death almost inevitable, the alternatives were carefully considered—to stay and die Armenian, or to go to America and die old."[89] The Garoghlanians, like the Saroyans, chose to emigrate and settled in Fresno, California, in the the San Joaquin Valley, a region geographically similar to southern Armenia but in every other way different from it. They speak Armenian, and the family is still patriarchal, with ultimate authority in the hands of Aram's grandfather, the Old Man. But the Armenian traditions are slowly being eroded, particularly among the children of Aram's generation. An early collection of these stories was in fact called *A Native American*.[90]

In "Old Country Advice to the American Traveler" an uncle, remembering the way things were back home, warns his nephew, who is about to take a trip by train, to beware of impostors, loose women, gamblers, and thieves: "One thing more, the old man said. When you go to bed at night, take your money out of your pocket and put it in your shoe. Put your shoe under your pillow, keep your head on the pillow all night, *and don't sleep*" (*Aram*, 189).

The nephew finds no impostors, loose women, gamblers, or thieves on the American train, but he tells his uncle that he took his advice. The uncle is pleased: "I am pleased that *someone* has profited by my experience" (*Aram*, 191).

What matters is that the uncle *believes* he has been useful. Most of the stories turn on believing something is true, whether or not it really is. The last story, "A Word to Scoffers," deals with Aram's cross-country bus trip to New York. One of his stops is Salt Lake City, where a missionary tells him he can be saved with "the gospel of Brigham Young." The man is not talking about the book of Mormon but about Brigham Young's wonderful ability to believe in everything from angels to polygamy. All that Aram must do, the missionary says, is change his attitude and start believing *everything*. On the bus a few minutes outside Salt Lake City, Aram finds he has indeed been converted. He doesn't need his "book-learning" now: "I was believing everything, left and right, as the missionary had said, and it's been that way with me ever since" (*Aram*, 220).

To believe can also mean being crazy—or at least acting in a way that makes people think one is crazy. The people who believe have their private visions of the world, very unlike the narrow views held by most of the "Americans" and by Aram's uncle Zorab, who is "practical and nothing else" (*Aram*, 7). The Garoghlanians, except for Zorab and one or two others, are all believers. Extraordinary things happen—at least in their imaginations—that redeem them from their poverty and isolation.

To be a "lunatic," as Saroyan wrote elsewhere, was not thought by Armenians to be a bad thing. To be a lunatic was to be *khent*, a word "used without scorn and in some cases with admiration, if not indeed with reverence." David of Sassoun was said to be *khent*, and Saroyan thought of himself as a combination of "the wise man, and the fool, or at any rate the lunatic" (*Chance*, 46). Certainly most of the Garoghlanians are *khent*.

Garoghlanian is the Armenian for "of the family of the dark sons." Aram's mother, Mariam, and his grandmother have only minor roles in the stories. It is "the dark sons" with whom Saroyan is concerned. Standing over all is the Old Man, irascible and domineering, who has a brother or brother-in-law (it is not clear which) named Garro, the man with precautions about train travel. The Old Man also has five sons: practical Zorab; Melik, who turns a track of desert into a pomegranate grove only to find that no one in America wants pomegranates (anyway, he "just liked the idea of planting trees and watching them grow" [*Aram*, 35]); Gyko, who studies Eastern philosophy and believes the strength of God is within him; Jorgi, who works only when he has to and sings and plays beautiful melancholy music on his zither; and Khosrove, who is thought by everyone except Aram to be crazy.

Khosrove may act crazy, but Aram knows he has his reasons. Khosrove's sons are not at all like him; they include Arak, who gets his way in school by being charming and well mannered, and Dikran, who reads all the time and becomes a great success as an orator even though what he has to say, as the Old Man points out, is nonsense. Among Aram's other cousins, Zorab's son Mourad is, like his uncle Khosrove, crazy in everyone's opinion but Aram's. Vask, like his uncle Jorgi, is considered a fool. The various types (crazy, foolish, practical, and so on) continue from generation to generation but not necessarily from father to son: "The distribution of the various kinds of spirit of our tribe had been from the beginning capricious and vagrant" (*Aram*, 7).

Mourad and Khosrove are the most interesting of the Garoghlanians. They are both assumed to be crazy, but their craziness leads in opposite directions. Mourad, on the one hand, is high-spirited, doing whatever he wants. In Armenian, in fact, his name means "aspiration" or "ambition." Khosrove, on the other hand, mourns a homeland he can never regain, and his behavior is incomprehensible to anyone who does not know that his sadness underlies everything he says. Khosrove sees all the Garoghlanians, and indeed all those who have lost their homelands, as "poor and burning orphans" (*Aram*, 206). His grief is too deep for any other tragedy to reach him. His son runs to the barbershop to tell him his house is burning. "This man Khosrove," writes Saroyan, "sat up in the chair and roared, It is no harm; pay no attention to it. The barber said, But the boy says your house is on fire. So Khosrove roared, Enough, it is no harm, I say" (*Aram*, 7).

The first story in the book, "The Summer of the Beautiful White Horse," contrasts these two men. Mourad steals a horse (or rather "borrows" one, since the Garoghlanians are known for their honesty). He eventually returns it, but before he does so, its owner (an Assyrian who, "out of loneliness, . . . learned to speak Armenian") complains to Khosrove about the apparent theft. "It's no harm," Khosrove shouts back. "What is the loss of a horse? Haven't we all lost the homeland?" (*Aram*, 12).

"My Cousin Dikran" similarly contrasts the Old Man with one of his American grandsons. Dikran's knowledge comes from books—the Old Man's comes from experience. When he is 11 Dikran gives a speech at school, "dramatic, well-uttered, intelligent, and terribly convincing," in which he proves that the First World War "had *not* been fought in vain" (*Aram*, 108). But in building his brilliant argument he has overlooked the incalculable horrors of the war.

"I must tell you I am rather pleased," his grandfather says. "A statement as large and as beautiful as that deserves to come only from the
lips of a boy of eleven—from one who believes what he is saying. From
a grown man, I must tell you, the horror of that remark would be just
a little too much for me to endure" (*Aram*, 109).

Like *Little Children, My Name Is Aram* is patterned on *Winesburg,
Ohio*.[91] The stories in both are related in tone and characters but remain
separate narrative units. Both books are interrelated stories of initiation
involving boys or young adolescents learning about the world. The
technique was also used by Mark Twain in *The Adventures of Huckleberry
Finn*, in which each episode as Huck and Jim travel down the river is
a separate, self-contained narrative, and in fact Saroyan cited Twain as
a major influence on his work (Basmadjian, 40). But Huck's relation to
others is very different from Aram's and from George Willard's in *Winesburg, Ohio*. Whereas at the end of Twain's novel Huck lights out for
"the territory" and freedom, at the end of *Winesburg, Ohio* George Willard is on his way to "his future life in the city"[92] and at the end of
Saroyan's book Aram, having just been taught by the missionary to
believe everything, is on his way to New York. Thus, whereas Twain
celebrates a frontier self-reliance, Anderson and Saroyan return always
to communities. For Saroyan, of course, this element is crucial: Aram
is defined in terms of family and Armenian heritage. He is certainly
not a Huck Finn. He leaves his home and goes to New York only
because one of his uncles says he should.

Saroyan's heroes invariably oppose institutional authority. It is that
opposition which, to use Khosrove's words, made the Armenians "poor
and burning orphans" (*Aram*, 206). But at the same time they are obedient to the authority of tradition and community—that is, to an authority that is not merely legislated and imposed.

It may be worth adding that Saroyan himself repeatedly had difficulties with institutional authorities—particularly, as is discussed later
in this volume, the IRS and the U.S. Army—but toward the end of his
life he moved back to the Armenian community in Fresno and listed
himself in the phone book as Aram Garoghlanian.

Saroyan's Fables (1941) was published in an edition of 1,000 copies,
and although Saroyan included two of the fables in *The Saroyan Special*
(1948), the book itself has never been reprinted.

Most of the book consists of traditional Armenian fables that Saroyan
had heard from one of his uncles, his grandmother, and others from

the old country. The fables are generally set in the Ottoman world, although the sultan is called the king, and in many the characters are explicitly or implicitly Armenians unwittingly caught in absurd situations. For example, the first fable in the book, a tale Saroyan says his grandmother told "to illustrate the awful loveliness of faith in God, and the absurdity of despair," deals with a carpenter ordered to deliver "eleven thousand eleven hundred and eleven pounds of fine hardwood sawdust for the king."[93] If he fails he will lose his life, but there is no way he can find so much sawdust. And so his friend convinces him that the best thing to do is forget everything, get drunk, and have a wonderful time, which he does. The next morning envoys from the king arrive not to arrest the carpenter but to order a coffin: the king is dead.

Fables were part of the Armenian folk tradition and, like *David of Sassoun*, were a way of mocking the Islamic rulers. One of the fables involves Ramazan, the Islamic time of fasting, which occurs each year during the ninth lunar month and ends when three men testify to having seen the new moon. It is followed by beiram, a period of feasting and joy. In the fable a deaf shepherd loses two sheep, one of which is crippled. They are found by a deaf townsman, who, proud of his family's reputation for honesty, tries to return them. The grateful shepherd offers the lame sheep as a reward, but the deaf townsman believes he is being accused of having crippled it. Meanwhile a deaf husband who has been fighting with his wife leaves home, intending never to return. The deaf shepherd and the deaf townsman encounter him and ask him to settle their dispute. He thinks they are trying to convince him to return to his wife. They argue with each other and finally take their cases before a deaf judge. "The deaf judge," the fable ends, "listened to the end, then announced loudly, Three of the Faithful have sworn that they have seen the new moon. Tell the villagers to fire the guns. *Ramazan* is ended. It is now *beiram*" (*Fables*, 47).

This fable is, of course, intended to make Moslems look foolish; everyone will now be celebrating beiram at the wrong time. But other, less obvious things are happening here. The only person in the story who is named is the townsman, who starts the chain of events. His name is Osman, and the historic Osman was the founder of the Ottoman dynasty—the man ultimately responsible for the Armenians' situation. The story says something about Ottoman "justice," too; the judge is deaf, as indeed provincial judges often were when Armenians were involved.

In another fable the king (or sultan) wants to find out how many blind people are in the city, and so one of his subjects drags a lilac branch through the streets. Whenever he is asked what he is doing, he knows the asker must be blind. The last person to ask is the king. Just as Ottoman judges were deaf, Ottoman sultans could be blind.

The fables take place in a world in which those without power must be cautious and not say more than is necessary. (One of the fables deals with Armenians who can "speak" with each other without using words.) A person had to be careful in a world of blind rulers and deaf judges—anything could happen. Sultan Abdul Hamid II, surely one of the most paranoid monarchs in modern history, found the formula H_2O in a chemistry textbook used by his Armenian subjects. He knew subversion when he saw it: the Armenians were telling one another that Hamid II was a zero.

Although publicized and reviewed as a novel, *The Human Comedy* (1943) can also be read as a series of interrelated short stories, such as those collected in *My Name Is Aram*.[94]

The Human Comedy, while set during the Second World War, is based on Saroyan's boyhood in Fresno a generation earlier. Both Homer Macauley and his kid brother, Ulysses, are versions of Saroyan himself—the former as a high school student, the latter as a recently orphaned four-year-old.[95] Like Homer, Saroyan worked as a messenger boy in the Fresno telegraph office, a job that gave him access to people's private lives.

Homer and, to a lesser degree, Ulysses are used to tie together an otherwise loosely related series of episodes. The telegrams Homer delivers give Saroyan the opportunity for a series of self-contained episodes or short stories involving various residents of Ithaca, the California town in which the book is set. Other episodes involve Ulysses's friends and family. The stories are also linked through references to Homer's brother Marcus, who is in the army. Homer delivers the telegrams from the War Department announcing that someone has been killed in battle, and at the end of the book it is the telegram announcing his brother's death that he has to bring home.

The Human Comedy was originally written as a screenplay for Metro-Goldwyn-Mayer. When it became evident that the film would not be produced the way he felt it should be, Saroyan asked Harcourt, Brace to publish the screenplay complete with technical directions. The editor Robert Giroux read and liked the screenplay but felt it would work better as a novel, and he convinced Saroyan to rewrite it that way. But despite the work's origin and Giroux's suggestion, Saroyan's background as a short story writer remains clear throughout *The Human Comedy*. Like *My Name Is Aram*, the book takes *Winesburg, Ohio* as its model, a series of distinct if related episodes. Howard Estherbrook, who wrote the final screen version, made the film less loosely episodic by eliminating several of the stories and developing others.

Ithaca is patterned on Fresno but has more to do with all-American towns MGM films traditionally idealized. Saroyan calls the place Ithaca because it is the home of so many "wanderers"—immigrants of Italian, Mexican, Greek, Irish, Armenian, and Polish extraction. There are a few "Americans," some of whom, as is usual in Saroyan's work, are mean-spirited or bigoted, but everyone else is united by common regard for the rights of others. Almost everyone in Ithaca is good; even Dolly Hawthorne, the local madam, turns out to be a sweet lady very concerned about the loneliness of soldiers and sailors away from home. Ithaca is another version of the America Norman Rockwell was illustrating for the *Saturday Evening Post.*

It is easy to criticize *The Human Comedy.* Most of the time Saroyan seems to be simply pleasing his audience, telling them only what they want to hear. He offers no difficult or troubling ideas; characterization is never subtle; the humor is broad; and the tone is usually genial and light. And yet Homer's job is to deliver "death messages," "telegrams of death." Homer has to support his family because his father is dead and Marcus is in the army. The book ends with Marcus's death and the death of Homer's friend Mr. Grogan, who works in the telegraph office. Life in Ithaca seems on the one hand placid and gentle but on the other always threatened by war and death.

The Human Comedy shares with Saroyan's best work a surface that tries to please but never fully hides the nightmares ready to break through. "The Daring Young Man," "Seventy Thousand Assyrians," "The Living and the Dead," "The Summer of the Beautiful White Horse," and other important stories never completely resolve their tensions between Saroyanesque sentiment and ideals on the one hand and dark inevitability on the other, but ultimately one senses that fate, not wishful thinking, is in charge. Sweetness and sentiment dominate *The Human Comedy,* however. Ithaca is Saroyan's utopia, a place where, sooner or later, things will work out for the best.

A case in point is the story entitled "The Holdup Man," in which Tom Spangler, who manages the telegraph office, convinces a young drifter to go home and settle down. Tom is the sort of man who can always find a person's decent side. "The graveyards and penitentiaries are full of good American kids who've had bad luck and hard times," he tells the drifter. "They're not criminals." The drifter listens to Tom's advice. "You needn't worry about me," he says at the end. "I'm going home where I belong. . . . And now I'm going to know *how* to live."[96]

In "The Apricot Tree" nine-year-old August ("Auggie") Gottlieb convinces the boys in his neighborhood gang to try to steal Mr. Henderson's apricots. The apricots aren't ripe, but Auggie steals one anyway just to show he can do it. Mr. Henderson chases the boys away, but he isn't really mad. The story is, of course, drawn from the episode in St. Augustine's *Confessions* in which he talks about having stolen pears as a boy, and that is why Auggie is called "the great religious leader" (and named Gottlieb) and why his followers are called "religious fanatics" (*Human*, 173, 175). But while Augustine used the incident as the basis for a long digression on guilt and sin, in Saroyan's fantasy the moral seems to be that boys will be boys.

In "Three Soldiers," "To Mother, with Love," and "It's Your Misfortune and None of My Own" Homer's sister, Bess, and Marcus's girlfriend, Mary Arena, are stopped on the way to the movies by three soldiers from out of town. One of them asks whether he and his buddies can go, too, and Bess and Mary decide that would be all right: after all, these men are just lonely. On the way to the theater the soldiers send telegrams home, and during the movie Bess talks about patriotism and her brother Marcus. As they leave the theater the soldiers kiss the girls and, as Mary and Bess turn to go home, play leapfrog, "pushing down the dark, immortal street nearer and nearer to the War."[97]

In the end one feels that Saroyan's utopia would probably be a terribly dull place to live: nothing remarkable is ever likely to happen. Aside from a few nasty people, such as the high school track coach, everyone is relentlessly courteous, unfailingly kind, and thoroughly average. Life is amusing rather than comic, sad rather than tragic. Virtue is rewarded, and endings are (mostly) happy.

Saroyan insisted that the book was not sentimental. The movie, he said, was, but that was only because "Americans" could not do what he did, and what was "natural" for him as an Armenian turned sentimental when they tried to do it themselves. What for them was sentimental was for him "disciplined longing" (Basmadjian, 43–44). Sentimentality, of course, is dishonest, involving a refusal to understand or feel deeply, and Saroyan implied that he hid or avoided nothing, that he was only "longing." Perhaps so, but *The Human Comedy* reads like the work of a clever craftsman reaching for his widest popular appeal. Aram Saroyan's account of his father as "essentially an *entertainer*" with a "bag of tricks" seems to fit the author of *The Human Comedy* (Aram Saroyan, 33, 35).

The book's excessive sentiment and sugary ideals may have had less to do with Saroyan than with the man for whom he was working, for *The Human Comedy* was written for Louis B. Mayer, the ruling head of MGM. Mayer was responsible for the Andy Hardy films, which received a special Academy Award in 1942 (the year Saroyan began work on the scenario) for "furthering the American way of life."[98]

Mayer loved *The Human Comedy* more than any other movie he made.[99] It perfectly expressed that ideal America which MGM films repeatedly portrayed throughout the depression and the war—an America in which Mayer fervently believed, a world of decent people and homespun truths in which virtue was always rewarded. Mayer was no intellectual, but he was a deeply emotional man, easily moved to tears, and no matter how often he saw the film he would start crying as soon as he saw the opening shots. Mayer's idea of great art was the Grandma Moses paintings with which he decorated the walls of his lavish Bel Air mansion, and it was that innocent America which found its way into the Andy Hardy films and *The Human Comedy.*

The Human Comedy, Neal Gabler has written, was "as close to an ultimate expression of the Mayer philosophy as one was likely to get"—a vision of the decent, small-town, patriotic America for which the war was being fought (Gabler, 388). Homer Macauley was played in the film by Mickey Rooney, America's favorite teenager, and once one has seen the film, it is difficult to imagine anyone but him in the part. Saroyan's biographers have suggested that in fact Arthur Freed, who first brought Saroyan and Mayer together, may have urged Saroyan to design *The Human Comedy* precisely for Rooney (Lee and Gifford, 64). The closer one examines either the book or the film, the less one finds of Saroyan, at least the Saroyan of *Inhale and Exhale* and *My Name Is Aram*, and the more one finds of Mayer and MGM.

Eventually Saroyan had his own reservations about the book. In 1961 he observed that when he wrote something popular, he had questions about what he had done and the reasons for its popularity. Two of his works, *My Name Is Aram* and *The Human Comedy*, had been hugely popular, and he had no question about the first: it could "do the reader no harm." But the second had "some lapses," particularly at the end, where death in battle could be seen as "a thing of great meaning."[100] He claimed he had written the passage that way because he had been under pressure.

Between 1943, when *The Human Comedy* was published, and 1950 Saroyan wrote comparatively little, aside from a novel, *The Adventures of Wesley Jackson*, and a few unsuccessful plays. *Dear Baby* was his last collection of short fiction until *The Assyrian* appeared in 1950.

There are several possible reasons for the sudden break in what had been (and would later again be) one of the most prolific careers in American writing. For one thing, there was an unhappy marriage that ended in divorce in 1949.[101] Other crises included problems with the IRS, repeated attacks on his work by academic and Eastern critics, and, following publication of *The Human Comedy*, his own private war with the U.S. Army. Of all his difficulties, he felt those with the military were the most traumatic (Basmadjian, 44).

In 1945 the *New York Times Magazine* carried an article entitled "Pvt. Saroyan and the War," reporting that William Saroyan was in London "on special assignments for a United States Army film unit." Saroyan shared an office with Pvt. Irwin Shaw, who was already well known as a writer, although not as well known as Saroyan. "The exact nature of their work," the article continued, "verges on a military secret, but it involves highly flexible hours and a large degree of freedom from the usual regimentation of Army life. They live in a flat on Pall Mall."[102]

How, one might ask, could a buck private afford an apartment on Pall Mall? Well, explained Saroyan, there were royalties from *The Human Comedy*. That book was so popular that it had been reissued in 1943 as a paperback in the Editions for the Armed Services series and the following year by Overseas Editions, Inc. It was a curious choice for a military publication, however, since it was implicitly an antiwar book and Saroyan had been a vociferous opponent of the draft and military servir

In part the popularity of *The Human Comedy* certainly had something to do with the film, though there were considerable differences between them, particularly in their attitudes to the war. In the movie Marcus Macauley and his army buddies are treated as heroes, and that was never what Saroyan intended. To him they were victims. Saroyan's attitude toward the war had been clear as early as *Inhale and Exhale*, in which he wrote, "So before the war starts (and everybody alive, from the cab driver to the Professor of Economics, at Columbia, will tell you the war will soon start), I want to tell the world that I am not interested. I am completely bored with the war. It has nothing to do with me. . . . I want nothing of it, I refuse to accept its reality" (*Inhale*, 414).

Many other comments of this sort appear in his early books, and less than a year after Pearl Harbor he produced his own antiwar play, *Across the Board on Tomorrow Morning*, on Broadway.[103] "I have been the best American propagandist this country ever had," Saroyan told the New York *Herald Tribune* at this time, "and I can't do more than I am doing by writing" (Lee and Gifford, 90). That in essence was what he also told the draft board, but it didn't agree and Saroyan was soon drafted. "He was absolutely violated by the fact that he had been drafted," his wife said many years later. "It was an agony for him" For one thing, "he didn't believe in the war," she said, but more significantly, for Saroyan there was "personal discomfort" in "having any regimented life of any kind" (Lee and Gifford, 95).

Saroyan's attitude toward the war is not so explicit in *The Human Comedy* (he was, after all, writing for Mayer), but it is unmistakably there. Ithaca would be a utopia were it not for the bureaucrats and generals who wage wars. But the film is narrated by Marcus's dead father, proud his son is fulfilling his patriotic duty. In three separate sequences Marcus is shown with his army buddies laughing and singing, and in the last of these they are headed for combat. There is no resistance, no sense that they are doing anything but what has to be done. The movie ends not with the Macauleys' grief but with the ghosts of father and son entering the Macauley house, future guardians of an ideal American home.

As the article in the *Times* suggests, Saroyan's military duties were in fact not very onerous. He never saw combat, and royalties allowed him to live much better than almost everyone else in the army. He had not opposed the war as strongly as, for example, Robert Lowell and William Everson, who declared themselves conscientious objectors and who went to prison rather than serve in the armed forces. But many years later, explaining why the experience had been so traumatic, Saroyan said that such experiences made an individual helpless (Basmadjian, 42).

Saroyan's one significant creative effort while he was in the army was an antiwar novel, *The Adventures of Wesley Jackson* (1945), a book for which he was universally criticized. Irwin Shaw in the *New York Times Book Review* pointed out that the only bad people in the book were not

German or Japanese but American. Saroyan "forgives the Germans Dachau and Belsen without blinking an eye," Shaw wrote, "but he cannot forgive the sergeant who assigned him to KP in New York City."[104] Edmund Wilson attacked the novel at length, claiming among other things that one of the chapters "contained some of the silliest nonsense ever published by a talented writer."[105] And Diana Trilling told her readers that the book was "a form of punishment" she could not recommend; the chapter headings alone would suffice for "even the most masochistic."[106]

Saroyan lost twice, first to the military and then to the critics. His early stories had been attacked by critics on the Left, but he had survived that, and his stories and plays in the late 1930s and 1940s had made him more famous than ever. By 1941 it seemed quite possible that no one had ever been published as widely as he. His work had appeared in very nearly every periodical of consequence in the country.[107] If nothing else, that was a sign of his popularity, and certainly he was a celebrity; still, there were many who had strong reservations about his work, and they included some very prominent critics.

As questions about Saroyan's politics faded, he was attacked on precisely those grounds for which he was most famous: the "Saroyanesque" style and the informality and freedom of his work. The critics were formalists; their idol was Henry James; and their attack was part of a general assault on all expressionist writers, from Whitman to Kerouac.

One of the first and most famous to turn on Saroyan was Edmund Wilson. In his study of California writers, "The Boys in the Back Room," originally published in the *New Republic* in 1940, Wilson argued that although Saroyan derived from Anderson and Hemingway, he had achieved much less than his masters. There were good things to be said about "The Living and the Dead," but in general Saroyan was like "a good drunk." He was not untalented, but at times it looked as if he might become "the kind of columnist . . . who merely turns on the tap every day and lets it run a column" (Wilson, 27, 29).

Wilson at least granted Saroyan a future as a columnist. Philip Rahv was somewhat less charitable. When in 1943 Rahv wrote a predominantly negative survey of Saroyan's work, he gave it the subtitle "A Minority Report," yet the minority for which he spoke was hugely influential in the universities. Saroyan was simply "an object lesson in the atrophy of taste and decay of values to which . . . [American] literature has been exposed since the early 1930s." The stories, excepting perhaps *The Daring Young Man* and very little else, simply did not measure up. Saroyan lacked "nearly all the primary elements of craft." Furthermore, Saroyan insisted (and this especially annoyed Rahv) on art as self-expression, a "notion" that "has long ago been discarded by the best modern thinking on the subject." Rahv wanted fiction in which the artist was obviously in control, and his pantheon of contemporary writers had no room for one who seemed to be "ad-libbing from start to finish."[108]

In his most famous essay, "Paleface and Redskin," Rahv opposed the party of Whitman (redskins) to the party of James (palefaces) and made clear his reservations about the first, in which category he included, among others, Hemingway ("that perennial boy-man"), Anderson, Wolfe, Steinbeck, and Saroyan.[109]

Depending on the critic, Saroyan was viewed as a good drunk, merely an ad-libber, or, in Diana Trilling's view, at times emotionally a child. Reviewing *Dear Baby* for the *Nation* in 1944, she concluded that Saroyan "arrests the mature world at the child level of childhood—a comforting act of fantasy but a debilitating one."[110]

Critical dogma in the academy, meanwhile, was represented by the New Critics, conservative formalists for whom the exuberant and seemingly shapeless ramblings of a Miller, Wolfe, or Saroyan were an anathema. In *Understanding Fiction* (1943) Cleanth Brooks and Robert Penn Warren presented fiction as something that conformed to a set of standards and categories. They emphasized objective control of form. The ghost of Percy Lubbock had returned.

A famous example of the new formalist thinking was Mark Schorer's frequently reprinted and widely admired article "Technique as Discovery," originally published in 1948. In that article Schorer specified Saroyan as one who had erred precisely because he had failed to acquire that formal control essential to a work of art. Responding to Elizabeth Bowen's claim that in D. H. Lawrence's work "every bush burns," Schorer said that "the bush burns brighter in some places than in others, and it burns brightest when a passionate private vision finds its objectification in exacting technical search." In Saroyan, by contrast, there was "no such objectification" and therefore only "a burning without a bush."[111]

Of all the fronts from which the critics attacked Saroyan and his expressionist aesthetics, perhaps none was more difficult to argue with than R. P. Blackmur's. Once he had laid down his own rules for critical combat, there was nothing his opponents could say. He ruled them out of literature before discussion began.

Blackmur's principal targets were Lawrence and Wolfe, but what he had to say reflected harshly on all expressionist writing. Blackmur opposed "expressive" to "objective" form. The latter, he said, provided a "rational structure which controls, orders, and composes in external or objective form the material of which it is made," whereas expressive form involved "the faith . . . that if a thing is only intensely enough felt its mere expression in words will give it satisfactory form, the dogma, in short, that once material becomes words it is its own best form."[112] Expressive form, he said in his critique of Wolfe's *From Death to Morning*, was a matter of "Write what you see, whatever it is, and say what you feel or ought to feel, and the thing will make itself a work of art."[113] Blackmur's reaction to expressive form was itself somewhat expressive: expressive form, he said, was a "plague" and a "heresy" (Blackmur 1935, 105; Blackmur 1940, 190).

Blackmur, Schorer, Brooks, Warren, and other New Critics created a climate of ideas in which Saroyan could not find a hearing: his work could be dismissed simply on technical grounds; literature was only what could be filtered through a sieve of critical assumptions. The situation was, however, literally academic, and the following decade saw a powerful reaction with the recognition among younger writers of Miller, Kerouac, Wolfe, and other expressionists. Saroyan benefited from that change, and new editions of his major works came out in the 1950s and the 1960s. Nonetheless, formalist criticism continued to have a powerful lingering effect among academics—a fact evident even now in the continued absence of almost all the expressionists, including Saroyan, from anthologies of American literature edited for college courses.

Regardless

The Assyrian and Other Stories (1950) collects Saroyan's short fiction from the 1940s. Although the title story is one of his more powerful, others in the collection (particularly "The Pheasant Hunter" and "The Third Day after Christmas") lack the energy that sustains his earlier work.

The book opens with a long introduction, "The Writer on the Writing," in which Saroyan restates his expressionist position. In general, he says, he had not written "*deliberately.*" Writing was not a matter of choice: it was something he had to do. "I was generally *impelled* to write," he says, "and whatever it turned out to be, it was O.K. as far as I was concerned because it was what I had been helpless not to write" (*Assyrian*, xvii).

But to do what he did best Saroyan needed freedom, and on several fronts—the military, the critical establishment, the IRS (now trying to collect more than $30,000 in back taxes), and his marriage and divorce—his life was now limited and defined by laws, institutions, and people over whom he had no control. "The voice was as loud as ever," his biographers report, "but the sureness was gone" (Lee and Gifford, 142). Saroyan's writing depended on a perfect self-assurance. As he said, he could not write deliberately, and doubting himself, he doubted the writing.

"The Pheasant Hunter" and "The Third Day after Christmas" fail because Saroyan cannot sustain the easy, graceful rhythms for which he was famous.[114] In both these stories he makes sudden, improbable shifts in narrative only to keep the prose moving, and the results are mechanical and forced. "The Assyrian" is among Saroyan's major works, but its tone is despair and loss. It is the confession of a writer who, at the end of the day, has a story containing none of the energy or power that a few years earlier he would have taken for granted.

Most of the stories in *The Assyrian* deal with failure or abandonment. In each the subject is a victim, someone who is not responsible for his or her predicament but who suffers for it and survives. Survival is something Saroyan had to learn early. When he was three, his father died. His mother sent him to an orphanage for the next six years, a fact so painful that he did not mention it in any of his work until 1952, three years after her death. Now, in the late 1940s, he was in a sense again abandoned and had to find ways to overcome his predicament.

Saroyan had always written about outsiders who survive emotionally and spiritually despite great odds. In many major stories that depends on the individual's sense of ethnic background, but in other important works survival can depend on imagination (for example, "The Daring Young Man"), emotional self-sufficiency ("The Trains"), luck ("The Man with His Heart in the Highlands"), and so forth. By the time *The Assyrian* was published, however, it seemed as if the only refuge was ethnic identity.

The title story is based on Saroyan's 1949 visit to Lisbon, where he met Calouste Gulbenkian, an Armenian entrepreneur who had amassed a fortune in shipping and oil.[115] At a time when everything seemed to have failed, Gulbenkian welcomed Saroyan as a fellow Armenian. This wealthy businessman was surrounded by enemies; even the waiters at his hotel were paid to overhear his conversations, and so he spoke in Armenian, a language none of the waiters understood. Saroyan and Gulbenkian shared a heritage and a language that protected them from a hostile world.

According to the introduction, "The Assyrian" was originally written to please editors. Saroyan needed money and began the story believing it would earn him between $15,000 and $25,000. But as he wrote, he found the material strangely intractable, refusing to conform to the kind of fiction that was popular and sought by editors.

The tone is somber and resigned. Both "The Daring Young Man" and "The Assyrian" are about the death of a writer, but while in the first the central character continues to live in his world of books, in the second an established, respected writer deserts his work and returns to the home of his ancestors. The choice was crucial and inevitable for Saroyan. His writing depended on his Armenian identity, and in a crisis that identity came first. But this choice may explain in part why his fiction at midcareer is, with the exception of a few stories like "The Assyrian," so weak. Under attack from all sides, Saroyan apparently withdrew into his sense of himself as Armenian rather than his sense of himself as a writer. "He had," as he said, "no heart for the work" (Lee and Gifford, 143).

Paul Scott in "The Assyrian" feels he has lost virtually everything—money, family, dignity. He has failed as a father, as a writer, and as a man. All that remains is his celebrity, and at the Portuguese hotel where he is living, that still counts for much. He is treated respectfully even when he cannot pay his bills: it is important for the hotel to have such a famous guest. Among others living there is Curti Urumiya, a wealthy Assyrian gentleman (based, of course, on Gulbenkian) who lives in self-imposed seclusion. He transacts his business and spends time with family and friends but remains spiritually and emotionally isolated. Within his solitude, however, his identity as an Assyrian is secure, and that is more significant to him than anything he has had to sacrifice. Scott is Assyrian on his mother's side, and Urumiya becomes in effect his spiritual father, leading him to an awareness of a heritage more valuable than anything he has lost.

"The Assyrian" reasserts Saroyan's belief in community, that central belief which distinguishes him from those American writers from Cooper to Twain who celebrate the individual. At the critical moment when everything seems to have failed, Paul Scott does not turn to his own resources (as even the daring young man had done) or to a frontier; instead he turns to the past and to the mystical sense of community that Curti Urumiya has shown him. Ethnic identity has assumed transcendent importance—an importance much greater than the self, the failures of which seem by comparison insignificant.

Many of the stories in *The Assyrian*, including "The Theological Student," "The Foreigner," and "The Parsley Garden," also deal with ethnic community and tradition; others depend merely on sudden good fortune for their resolutions but do not work. In "The Pheasant Hunter," for example, a father buys a gun for his son and then, since there are no pheasants in the part of the country where his son goes to hunt, sits back waiting to ridicule him when he returns home empty-handed. But the boy meets a man who understands that pride is at stake and who thus buys a couple of pheasants from a local restaurant for the boy to bring to his father. In "The Third Day after Christmas" a father deserts his son outside a bar. The bartender at first tries to make the boy go away but, when it is clear the father will not return, takes him home.

"The Poet at Home" is about a failed writer, Ralph Gallop, known, where he is known at all, as the author of one of the least successful plays ever produced on Broadway. But then he writes a play that does succeed—although, improbably, when he sees it performed he doesn't recognize it as his own, and his wife conspires to keep the truth from him. Though he is a cheerful, humorous person, his humor is his way of compensating for his failures. His wife knows success could change him, and she wants to keep him the way he is. The story, then, is about the way a man's wife will manipulate him to make him what she wants. Ultimately the point is to excuse a man from his sense of personal failure: he is not a failure—it is only that wives make men feel that way.

Like Paul Scott, Andrew Loring in "The Cocktail Party" is a writer whose private life has been a series of failures. He attends a cocktail party given by his former wife, and there he talks for the first time in many years with his son. The son, who wants to be a writer, has read and is enthusiastic about his father's work. The central point of Loring's books, the son realizes, is that people don't choose to be what they are: they are forced by circumstances to do things they would never do if they had the freedom to decide for themselves.

"The Pheasant Hunter," "The Third Day after Christmas," "The Poet at Home," and "The Cocktail Party" are desperate stories, the work of a writer who can no longer resolve his characters' dilemmas except in fortuitous and improbable ways. "The Poet at Home" and "The Cocktail Party" also seem self-serving, excusing their heroes for shortcomings Saroyan may well have found in himself. The stories in *The Assyrian* work only when they evoke a mystic bond between ancestors and descendants, a transcendent identity that cannot be altered by circumstance.

As he grew older, Saroyan increasingly took on the appearance of an Armenian patriarch, and later photographs showing the stout, bemused Saroyan with his great handlebar mustache are very different from the image of the brash, self-confident young man he had projected in the thirties and early forties. Confronted with failures in his own life, Saroyan remade himself in the image of his ancestors. Then he was able to write again as prolifically and, at times, as well as he had done earlier.

In the end Saroyan became a cultural figure of enormous prominence within the Armenian community. On his death in 1981, half his ashes were buried in Fresno, while the other half, as he had wished, were taken to Soviet Armenia and entombed in the Pantheon, a shrine set aside for the ashes of the most distinguished people of Armenian heritage.

In 1956 Saroyan published *The Whole Voyald and Other Stories*, the last miscellaneous collection of short fiction published in his lifetime. As in his earlier collections, the volume contains many pieces that are closer to essays than traditional stories. "A Writer's Declaration," for example, is a long, rambling work, partly anecdotal, in which Saroyan brings together various memories and observations from his career as a writer. It is another attempt to define his aesthetics and is important as such, but few except Saroyan himself would call it a story.

"The Winter Vineyard Workers" brings together various aspects of Saroyan's expressionist aesthetics. The story is set in California during Saroyan's boyhood years and concerns a Japanese laborer named Ito. Ito tells his fellow workers, among whom is the narrator, that he once killed a friend who had cheated him at cards. He did it, he says, not just for revenge but because he is by nature *"baggarro,"* a Japanese word literally meaning "crazy" but suggesting "sorrowful" as well. The other workers try to convince Ito that he had other reasons, but he insists that, no, it was only his nature, *baggarro.* Because of what he has done, he has also never married, feeling that anyone who has killed "cannot be a father."

Sometime later the narrator shows Ito reproductions of watercolors by José Clemente Orozco. Ito is fascinated by one that shows a man raging at his terrified children and wife. Something in the picture, the narrator says, suggests that the rage, whatever its source, has nothing to do with its victims: "one felt that it was for everything and everybody, *except* them."[116] After studying the man and the picture for a while, Ito concludes, *baggarro.*

"The Winter Vineyard Workers" is about the kind of fundamentally ahistorical force that Saroyan wanted his work to express. There is no reason, no cause, for Ito's *baggarro*; it is in his blood, and its force cannot be denied. He understands it in language peculiar to his ethnic heritage—a word than cannot be adequately translated—but it can be found as clearly in the work of a Mexican artist. Similarly, whatever it was Saroyan called "Armenian" (or "Assyrian") had its expression in all cultures. Criticized for having made Paul Scott an Assyrian rather than an Armenian, Saroyan said maybe that was a mistake "but not really, because in a sense everybody in the world is an Assyrian" (*Letters*, 42).

Much of the work in *The Whole Voyald* is explicitly autobiographical, and indeed memoir, rather than fiction, was Saroyan's characteristic mode during the final years of his career. Although in "The Assyrian" he had resolved his various crises by reaffirming that what matters is ethnic, not personal, identity, he began now to write more directly about his private experience. It was as if he were able to indulge freely in the vocabulary and rhythms of his personal voice only after he had convinced himself and his audience that he spoke principally as an Armenian.

"The Home of the Human Race," "Love of London," "The Idea in the Brother's Head," and other "stories" in *The Whole Voyald* are actually memoirs and reflective pieces about Saroyan's past. They are not fiction. Names and facts are correctly reported. At points they are almost journalistic. How is this kind of work different from works like *Places Where I Have Done Time*—that is, works being published at this time but advertised as memoirs? The distinction seems to have to do more with the way the books were sold than with the way they were written.

The first strictly autobiographical book Saroyan published was the journal he kept while writing *The Adventures of Wesley Jackson*. Journal and novel were issued in one volume as *The Twin Adventures* in 1950. As Irwin Shaw pointed out in his review of *Wesley Jackson*, Saroyan's hero and Saroyan himself were not easily distinguishable from each other, except in the chapters set in Germany, where Saroyan had never been (Shaw, 1). The journal simply reinforced the impression that the novel in effect was largely a memoir.

Two years after *The Twin Adventures* Saroyan published *The Bicycle Rider in Beverly Hills* (1952), dealing in part with some of the more painful aspects of his childhood, and followed it with nearly a dozen books that are either autobiography or collections of informal essays involving his personal observations and prejudices: *Here Comes There Goes You Know Who* (1961), *Not Dying* (1963), *After Thirty Years* (1964), *Short Drive, Sweet Chariot* (1966), *I Used to Believe I Had Forever, Now I'm Not So Sure* (1968), *Days of Life and Death and Escape to the Moon* (1970), *Places Where I've Done Time* (1972), *Sons Come and Go, Mothers Hang in Forever* (1976), *Chance Meetings* (1978), *Obituaries* (1979), and *Births* (1983).

Many of these books involve a gimmick that is essentially little more than an excuse for writing. In *After Thirty Years*, for example, Saroyan decided to write a book in exactly the length of time it had taken to write *The Daring Young Man* and to talk only about his experiences writing it. *Places Where I've Done Time* is a series of pieces about places where he had lived or visited; *Obituaries* concerns people he knew or knew about who died in 1976. What matters in each case is the ongoing fact of writing, and the memoir or informal essay serves much the same function as the short story had earlier.

* * *

Considering that Saroyan had once been known primarily for his short stories, there is surprising little that can be classified as such in the last 30 years of his career. *My Kind of Crazy, Wonderful People: Seventeen Stories and a Play* (1966) does not, strictly speaking, contain new work; rather, it includes earlier stories—"Antranik of Armenia," "The Daring Young Man," and so forth—rewritten as "plays." Narrative and discursive passages have been removed, and what remains has been divided into "scenes," with a list of characters and "setting" for each. This curious book was lavishly produced and heavily illustrated. Yet the stories themselves gain nothing from their new arrangement, and the book is rarely mentioned by Saroyan's biographers and critics.

I Used to Believe I Had Forever, Now I'm Not So Sure (1968) is generally listed among Saroyan's collections of short stories, although this miscellaneous collection of reviews, essays, commentary, and so forth seems uncomfortable there, even conceding Saroyan's broad definition of "story." A better argument can be made for *Letters from 74 rue Taitbout*, also listed among the short stories, for although the book deals largely with Saroyan's past, particularly people he has met, the "letters" were never intended to be sent.[117] Rather they provided an excuse for opinions and anecdotal reminiscences.[118]

Some of the letters deal with celebrities Saroyan had known, but the best are those concerned with the Armenian diaspora. There is, for example, a letter to Dikran Saroyan, who wanted to return to Armenia, though no one knew why. Perhaps it was simply because he was homesick; perhaps he thought if he went back, doing so would somehow cure his tuberculosis. But no one knew for sure, and his strange odyssey came to an end with his death in Constantinople, before he reached home. Although his motivations remained obscure, his failure to reach the homeland in order to be cured of whatever physical or psychological pain tormented him is symbolic of the finality of the loss of the homeland—a place to which one cannot return.

Another letter is addressed to Saroyan's cousin Hovagim: "You came to America, to work, to send money to your wife, so she and your sons could come too, but it didn't work out that way. You sent money and letters, and your wife replied, and then she didn't reply, and a whole year went by, and then another whole year went by, and you didn't know what had happened. You had an idea, but you didn't know for sure. You were alone everywhere I ever saw you" (*Letters*, 23–24).

On his deathbed Saroyan's grandfather had ordered his wife, "Get the family out of here, leave this place, go anywhere else, but do not stay here any longer, go to America if you can manage" (*Letters*, 24). Hovagim had not got his family out in time. "Your wife and two sons were in Bitlis," the letter says, "or near there or far from there, if they weren't dead, if they hadn't been killed, or hadn't died of hunger and thirst on the long march from Bitlis to the desert which so many others made and in which so many died. . . . Perhaps the boys were alive, but didn't know who they were, having been too little to remember, having been taken to an orphanage and given new names" (*Letters*, 23).

One of the stories collected in *The Whole Voyald* (1956), "The Home of the Human Race," is a long reflective piece concerned with Saroyan's memories of lonely people he had known as a boy. One of them is Hovagim Saroyan, again shown mourning his lost wife and sons, although here Saroyan wrote simply that "the wife had died, and the sons had gone along to her father's house. Thus, he was alone in California" (*Voyald*, 17). No mention is made of orphanages and forgotten identities or of the long march to the Syrian desert. "The Home of the Human Race" evokes a sense of gentle melancholy or pathos very different from the horror evoked by the account in *Letters from 74 rue Taitbout*.

Letters from 74 rue Taitbout was the last collection of new short fiction published in Saroyan's lifetime. There were, however, numerous reprints of earlier collections, particularly of *My Name Is Aram*, and in the last two decades of his life he worked on two series of short stories, collected posthumously by Leo Hamalian in *Madness in the Family* (1988). The less interesting of these involves divorce, the breakdown of families, and children caught between mutually hostile parents. In all these stories the father is exonerated, and his wife does not understand what her children need. There are very good moments in all these stories, particularly "Gaston," in which a father communicates with his daughter on a level of high whimsy. But even here everything conspires against making the wife seem fully human. Women in these stories are deceitful, silly, capricious, or superficial—never, in any case, a match for their good-humored, long-suffering husbands.

The other series, however, belongs among Saroyan's best work. It concerns the Bashmanians, immigrant Armenians like the Garoghlanians. In the title story Uncle Vorotan Bashmanian decides that until someone in the family has been buried in American soil, the family will remain exiles and wanderers. Whenever a relative is sick, he hurries to the bedside, hoping there will be a turn for the worse. Finally a death occurs, and Uncle Vorotan, greatly relieved, is cured of his obsession. The Bashmanians have a place in the New World, and he is free to go back to the more ordinary business of his life.

The Bashmanian stories are amusing, but, like all Saroyan's major works, they take place in a world of threats and suffering. In "Fire," Uncle Gunyaz Bashmanian burns his house to collect the insurance and pay his overdue bills. After setting the fire he sits down under a nearby fig tree for a wonderful Armenian dinner. He is philosophical and calm; tragedy is unavoidable. The fire, says the narrator, one of Gunyaz's nephews, "was the most beautiful, the most intelligent, the most artful, the sweetest, and the most philosophic . . . I ever saw." (*Madness*, 8).

Toward the end of his life Saroyan told an interviewer that he considered "Cowards," another in the Bashmanian series, to be one of his best stories (Basmadjian, 45). Written during the Vietnam conflict, it is among Saroyan's strongest antiwar pieces. It deals with Kristofor Agbadashian, who hides in his mother's home during the First World War. Others are killed in battle or die from other causes while serving their country, but he survives and becomes a father. One of his relatives points out that it is harder to be a coward than a soldier: "Coward he was, no doubt, but how much more brave a man must be to be a coward. It is easy to be a soldier of the government with all of your comrades. But it is very hard to be yourself, all alone under the bed in your mother's house" (*Madness*, 71). When a government investigator locates Kristofor after the war, it is only to close out all charges against deserters. If the record said "coward" Kristofor would have to be tried in court, and so the investigator simply writes down "father" and lets it go at that.

Hamalian wisely chose to conclude *Madness in the Family* with "The Duel," a story that echoes "A Fist Fight for Armenia," one of Saroyan's first published stories.[119] In the earlier story, during a fight between American and Armenian boys, a woman on the American side attacks the Armenians with, "You just watch. We'll cut you to pieces the way the Turks did." "These words sunk into Caspar's being," Saroyan wrote, "destroying him. The Turks were all right. They were fine. They were his neighbors, his brothers. He did not hate them. He loathed what was ugly in the woman's voice, the hideousness, the deformity she impelled in the earth" ("Fist Fight," 42).

In "The Duel" a boy named Trash Bashmanian learns how to fence but then needs an enemy with whom to fight. He decides that his enemy has to be a Turk, but there are no Turks in town. Meanwhile he has also become the leading schoolboy orator by preaching equality and brotherhood. How could anyone who preaches brotherhood hate Turks, let alone fight them? Finally his cousin, the story's narrator, takes fencing lessons too, "so that now and then we could take turns being the Turk in the world, and in our own hearts, each of us winning and losing every time, whichever side we took" (*Madness*, 141).

What had happened between Armenians and Turks was like a fight between cousins, neither one better than the other. Saroyan consistently refused to hate Turks for what had happened in Armenia. This was not simply a generous act on his part but the natural extension of his belief, discussed earlier, that, although there are genuinely cruel people like the American woman in "A Fist Fight for Armenia," the greater guilt belongs to institutions, governments, bureaucracies. "I kept wondering what had made [the Saroyans] all so alone, even when many of us were together," Saroyan wrote, "and what it was, I felt, was at least partly the people with power, with the papers, with the rubber stamps, the enforcers of the rules and regulations, a whole world full of such people. They scare a man. They are killers" (*Letters*, 25–26).

In *The Whole Voyald* Saroyan wrote that he had once wanted "to revolutionize American writing"; however, "for the most part my writing influenced unpublished writers who remained unpublished, and to measure that kind of an influence calls for a lot of imagination and daring. The good writers that my writing influenced were already published, some of them long published, but the truth is that my writing *did* influence their writing, too, for I began to notice the improvement almost immediately" (*Voyald*, 11). In fact Saroyan's fiction had considerable influence on writers as different as J. D. Salinger and Budd Schulberg, but his most important influence was on Jack Kerouac and, through him, a new generation of expressionist writers.[120]

In an essay entitled "The Great Rememberer" John Clellon Holmes wrote, "I imagined him (a lightning typist since his youth) sitting at the machine, staring into the blankness of the space in front of him, careful not to *will* anything, and simply recording the 'movie' unreeling in his mind. Somehow the words were no longer words, but had become things. Somehow an open circuit of feeling had been established between his awareness and its object of the moment, and the result was as startling as being trapped in another man's eyes."[121] In this passage Holmes is describing his friend Jack Kerouac, but without changing a word it could describe the young Saroyan. Kerouac first read Saroyan when, at age 18, he was trying to master the craft of writing. As he told Ted Berrigan many years later, the senior writer "got me out of the 19th century rut I was trying to study."[122] Kerouac instead began writing "little terse short stories in that general style" which Saroyan shared with Hemingway.[123] Although the principal influence on Kerouac's first novel, *The Town and the City* (1950), was Thomas Wolfe, that novel contains many distinctly Saroyanesque passages.[124] Still, Saroyan's greatest influence can be seen not in those passages but in the aesthetic principles that Allen Ginsberg called "spontaneous bop prosody" and that underlie *The Subterraneans, Desolation Angels, Visions of Cody*, and other works.

It is tempting to look for the origins of Kerouac's aesthetics in Charles Olson's essay "Projective Verse," but Kerouac insisted that he "formulated the theory of breath as measure, in prose and verse, never mind what Olson, Charles Olson says, I formulated that theory in 1953 at the request of [William S.] Burroughs and Ginsberg" (Berrigan, 555). Ginsberg agreed, saying that Kerouac was actually "following Charlie Parker, and also following Thomas Wolfe, and Saroyan—and Proust, and Céline"—in other words, jazz and prose narrative.[125]

According to Kerouac's "Essentials of Spontaneous Prose," the essay in which he summarized his aesthetic beliefs, a writer should seek "[n]ot 'selectivity' of expression but following free deviation (association) of mind into limitless blow-on-subject seas of thought, swimming in sea of English with no discipline other than rhythms of exhalation and expostulated statement."[126] This view is very close to Saroyan's sense of writing as something as natural and immediate as breathing. Kerouac said he got the idea for "spontaneous prose" from letters from his friend Neal Cassady. Nevertheless, Cassady was only doing what Saroyan had been doing for years—as Kerouac, having read Saroyan as closely as he did, must have known.

One interesting parallel between Saroyan and Kerouac is their respective debts to jazz. *On the Road*, as Warren Tallman has said, moves according to jazz rhythms,[127] and, as we have seen, it is jazz that underlies much of Saroyan's early work. But for Saroyan, of course, jazz meant something very different from what it meant for Kerouac. In Saroyan's generation the great musicians were Fats Waller, Bix Beiderbecke, Louis Armstrong, and so forth, whereas Kerouac and his contemporaries listened to bop musicians like Charlie Parker and Lester Young. However different the sound, there was in both that essential trust in improvisation, spontaneity, rhythmical complexity, and personal expression that is as much a part of *Inhale and Exhale* as *Visions of Cody*.

Not everyone saw Saroyan's influence on Kerouac as a good thing, particularly when they found in the younger writer the same sentimental qualities they disliked in his master. Henry Miller was delighted with Kerouac and wrote to Lawrence Durrell about him, but Durrell was less impressed, responding that "Saroyan has killed himself as a writer in this genre, the breathless lisp of a sweet little boy who is granted all the wonderful, wonderful treasures of God's own landscape. It is fundamentally pretentious—sentimental."[128] Readers who objected to Saroyanesque sentimentality and self-indulgence would also dislike Kerouac's celebration of the sad sweetness of being alone in America at night or the self-indulgence imbedded in such passages as "the raggedy madness and riot of our actual lives, our actual night, the hell of it, the senseless nightmare road."[129]

But if Kerouac inherited Saroyan's faults he also gained the ability to weave emotionally and musically complex sentences—the ability to transform prose into lyrical song: "Goodbye Cody—your lips in your moments of self-possessed thought and new found responsible goodness are as silent, make as least a noise, and mystify with sense in nature, like the light of an automobile reflecting from the shiny silver-paint of a sidewalk tank this very instant, as silent and all this, as a bird crossing the dawn in search of the mountain cross and the sea beyond the city at the end of the land."[130]

While beat writers, as Lawrence Lipton wrote, sought out "Saroyan's early short stories . . . in yellowing paperbacks," Saroyan himself seems to have paid little attention to the new generation.[131] In his introduction to David Kherdian's *Six Poets of the San Francisco Renaissance* he claimed never to have read the works of those whom Kherdian discussed, including Michael McClure and Brother Antoninus (William Everson), both of whom were clearly within the expressionist tradition.[132]

Saroyan was a writer caught between generations. Too young to have been part of the great avant-garde represented by Anderson, Hemingway, Stein, and others, he was too old to be part of the generation that gathered around Kerouac. With such notable exceptions as Miller and Wolfe, prominent writers who began to publish in the 1930s and 1940s were more concerned with being politically correct or with matters of technique than with the expressive possibilities of language and the Revolution of the Word.

Elizabeth Bowen felt that "probably since O. Henry nobody has done more than William Saroyan to endear and stabilize the short story, as it were, to guarantee it, to rescue it from its two extremes of possible disrepute—that of being purely esthetic, divorced from life, or purely commercial, divorced from virtue."[133] Bowen may be claiming too much for Saroyan; certainly there are those who would say that Anderson or Hemingway, for example, did as much or more. Nonetheless, it is surely true that Saroyan at his best had tried to steer the short story, or writing in general, away from the restrictions of the formalists while avoiding the pitfalls of mere commercialism. Saroyan, Bowen concluded, was one "who has never sold out—the inspired, sometimes flamboyant alien" (Bowen, 18). That is certainly the least that can be said about one who believed "the writer is a spiritual anarchist" and "the compulsion of our time" is "to become free" (*Voyald*, 12).

And freedom as a writer meant freedom from conventions and definitions and rules—freedom from even such distinctions as "fiction" and "essay." Critics and the past did not determine what a writer should do. There were no authorities. The great critical arguments in Saroyan's generation swirled around questions of what a writer should say and how he or she should say it—the form his or her fiction should take. Addressing young, beginning writers, Saroyan ignored all such critical labyrinths and concluded, "If a man says twenty words that are fresh and genuine, these words *are themselves form*" ("American Qualities," 47).

Notes to Part 1

1. The Armenian world can be traced back roughly to the time Greece emerged from the Dark Ages and the *Iliad* was written. It was then that the Armenians invaded and claimed as their homeland a massive stretch of the easternmost reaches of the Anatolian plateau and the southern Caucausus. They repeatedly tried to assert political independence, but during much of the succeeding 1,500 years they were successively ruled by Persians, Greeks, Seleucids, Romans, and Byzantines. The Ottoman Turks began invading Armenia in the early fifteenth century and, within 100 years, occupied it entirely. It remained part of the Ottoman Empire until the early years of this century.

The Armenians were initially considered by their Ottoman rulers to be *rayahs* (literally, sheep) to be protected. They, like Jews and other Christians, were "people of the book" who did not possess the full truth as revealed through Muhammad in the Koran. Ottoman rule was at first supposed to be benign (as if a father were dealing with recalcitrant children), but in practice things did not usually work out that way. Laws were passed making it illegal, for example, for Armenians to ride horses, plead their own cases in courts of law, or carry arms. Furthermore, they were required each winter to house any Kurd (the Kurds were Islamic) who paid a small fee to the local Ottoman official. Without guns or real possibilities for legal redress, the Armenians were entirely at the mercy of their "guests."

Armenians had certain freedoms and opportunities under the empire, but the legal, political, and economic restrictions were vast. Their language, church, and culture survived only at the mercy of the Ottoman state, and it should surprise no one that in Saroyan's work, criticism of political and social authority is immediate and reflexive.

2. For the sake of brevity, this story is henceforth referred to as "The Daring Young Man."

3. "Mr. Saroyan's Performance," *Nation*, 7 November 1934, 41.

4. Otis Ferguson, "That Performing Young Man," *New Republic*, 7 November 1934, 372.

5. *The Assyrian and Other Stories* (New York: Harcourt, Brace, 1950), xxiv; hereafter cited in text as *Assyrian*.

6. "Short Story," in *Cassell's Encyclopedia of Literature*, ed. S. H. Steinberg (London: Cassell, 1953), 504.

7. *The Daring Young Man on the Flying Trapeze and Other Stories* (New York: Random House, 1934), 32; hereafter cited in text as *Daring*.

8. The adjective was invented by Edmund Beloin in a parody of the Saroyan style, "Saroyanesque," *New Republic*, 26 December 1934, 201–2.

9. Ian Hamilton, *In Search of J. D. Salinger* (New York: Random House, 1988), 54.

10. Budd Schulberg, *The Four Seasons of Success* (Garden City, N.Y.: Doubleday, 1972), 58.

11. Quoted in Artine Artinian, *Maupassant Criticism in France: 1880–1940* (New York: King's Crown Press, 1941), 179.

12. See the introduction to Charles E. May, ed., *Short Story Theories* (n.p.: Ohio University Press, 1976), 6: "Although these same three complaints about the short story—lack of plot, lack of social concern, lack of ideology—have continued up through the sixties, in the last thirty years the critics have recognized that the short story is closer to the lyric than the novel and must be judged accordingly." See also in this volume Eileen Baldeshwiler, "The Lyric Short Story: The Sketch of a History," 202–13.

13. Sherwood Anderson, *A Story Teller's Story* (New York: B. W. Huebsch, 1924), 360.

14. James Schevill, *Sherwood Anderson: His Life and Work* (Denver, Colo.: University of Denver Press, 1951), xiii.

15. See, for example, Lionel Trilling, "Sherwood Anderson," in *The Liberal Imagination* (New York: Viking Press, 1950): 24–32.

16. Ray Lewis White, ed., *Sherwood Anderson/Gertrude Stein* (Chapel Hill: University of North Carolina Press, 1972), 82.

17. Gertrude Stein, review of *A Story Teller's Story*, in *Sherwood Anderson: A Collection of Critical Essays*, ed. Walter B. Rideout (Englewood Cliffs, N.J.: Prentice-Hall, 1974), 86. The review was originally published in 1925.

18. Anderson and German expressionism have a common ancestor in Whitman, whose poetry Saroyan considered the real root of American literature. For Whitman's importance to German expressionists, see Reinhold Grimm and Henry J Schmidt, "Foreign Influences on German Expressionist Poetry," in *Expressionism Reconsidered: Relationships and Affinities*, ed. Gertrud Bauer Pickar and Karl Eugene Webb (München: Wilhelm: Wilhame Fink Verlag, 1979), 9–18, and Roy F. Allen, *German Expressionist Poetry* (Boston: G. K. Hall, 1979).

19. R. S. Furness, *Expressionism* (London: Methuen, 1973), 1, 14.

20. Roger Asselineau, *The Transcendental Constant in American Literature* (New York: New York University Press, 1980), 134.

21. Hilaire Hiler, *Why Abstract?* (New York: New Directions, 1945), 10.

22. *Sherwood Anderson's Memoirs*, ed. Ray Lewis White (Chapel Hill: University of North Carolina Press, 1969), 21.

23. *After Thirty Years* (New York: Harcourt, Brace & World, 1964), 106–7; hereafter cited in text. See also "The Symphony," in *Inhale and Exhale* (New York: Random House, 1936).

24. Review of Michael Fanning, *France and Sherwood Anderson*, *New York Times Book Review*, 15 August 1976, 3.

25. Percy Lubbock, *The Craft of Fiction* (London: Jonathan Cape, 1921).

26. It was published in the February 1934 issue of *Story* and won the O. Henry Award that year.

27. William Saroyan, *Those Who Write Them and Those Who Collect Them* (Chicago: Black Archer, 1936), unpaged. Wolfe's response to Saroyan was less friendly. He wrote that Saroyan would never be a great writer until he got himself out of whatever he wrote—a strange comment from a writer whose books are themselves autobiographical and expressionist. (See Andrew Turnbull, *Thomas Wolfe* [New York: Charles Scribner's Sons, 1967], 253.)

28. Linda M. Wagner, "Modern American Literature: The Poetics of the Individual Voice," in *American Modern: Essays in Fiction and Poetry* (Port Washington, N.Y.: Kennikat Press, 1980), 96.

29. Quoted in Lionel Trilling, *Sincerity and Authenticity* (Cambridge, Mass.: Harvard University Press, 1972), 119.

30. Whit Burnett and Hallie Burnett, *The Modern Short Story in the Making* (New York: Hawthorn Books, 1964), 224.

31. Michael Stephens, *The Dramaturgy of Style: Voice in Short Fiction* (Carbondale and Edwardsville: Southern Illinois University Press, 1986), 7.

32. Robert Creeley, introduction to Charles Olson, *Selected Writings* (New York: New Directions, 1966), 9.

33. "Resurrections of a Life," in *Inhale and Exhale*, 3; hereafter cited in text as *Inhale*.

34. Gertrude Stein, "Poetry and Grammar," in *Lectures in America* (Boston: Beacon Press, 1985), 235. The lecture was originally published in 1935.

35. "Poem, Story, Novel," in *Inhale and Exhale*, 285.

36. Quoted in Lois Rather, *Gertrude Stein and California* (Oakland, Calif.: Rather Press, 1974), 77.

37. Amiel was very important to Saroyan as a writer, and later autobiographical works like *Days of Life and Death and Escape to the Moon* (1970) owe much to Amiel's example. That book opens with a series of quotations from Amiel's journal and includes a long passage in which Saroyan discusses his initial impressions of the book and its general value for him.

38. "What Makes American Writing American?" in *I Used to Believe I Had Forever Now I'm Not So Sure* (New York: Cowles, 1968), 134–40; hereafter cited in text as *I Used to Believe*.

39. Including, in Whitman's case, words heard in the street, political rhetoric, journalism, and bel canto opera.

40. Edward Foster, "An Armenian Poet in Istanbul," *Ararat* 28 (Winter 1987): 42.

41. Margaret Bedrosian, "William Saroyan and the Family Matter," *MELUS* 2 (Winter 1982): 13, 22.

42. James Joyce, *A Portrait of the Artist as a Young Man* (New York: Viking Press, 1964), 253.

43. Barbara Rose, *American Art since 1900*, rev. ed. (New York: Praeger Publishers, 1975), 126.

44. "The Armenian & the Armenian," in *Inhale and Exhale*, 438.

45. "The Revolution of the Word" was the motto of *transition* magazine, but the phrase covers the general modernist revolution in language exemplified by the work of Gertrude Stein, James Joyce, Ezra Pound, and others. See *Revolution of the Word*, ed. Jerome Rothenberg (New York: Seabury Press, 1974).

46. Saroyan also wrote to the Soviet journal *International Literature*, saying that as far as he was concerned, "a writer is exactly as important as the fellow who sweeps up horse-manure and dumps it into a can and sometimes a lot less interesting." (Quoted in Daniel Aaron, *Writers on the Left: Episodes in American Literary Communism* [New York: Harcourt Brace Jovanovich, 1961], 307.)

47. Malcolm Cowley, *The Dream of the Golden Mountains: Remembering the 1930s* (New York: Viking Press, 1980), 246.

48. Letter to the editors, *New Masses*, 23 October 1934, 15.

49. Editorial note, *New Masses*, 23 October 1934, 15.

50. Christina Stead, "The Impartial Young Man," *New Masses*, 17 March 1936, 24–25.

51. *Three Times Three* (Los Angeles: Conference Press, 1936), 70; hereafter cited in text as *Three*.

52. Edmund Wilson, "The Boys in the Back Room," in *Classics and Commercials: A Literary Chronicle of the Forties* (New York: Farrar, Straus, 1950), 29; hereafter cited in text. "The Boys in the Back Room" was originally published as a series of articles in 1940, when *Three Times Three* was still controversial.

53. James Burkhart Gilbert, *Writers and Partisans: A History of Literary Radicalism in America* (New York: John Wiley & Sons, 1968), 111.

54. William Phillips, *A Partisan View: Five Decades of the Literary Life* (New York: Stein & Day, 1983), 95.

55. Philip Rahv, "Narcissus," *Partisan Review* 2 (June 1935): 84–86.

56. Philip Rahv, "The Cult of Experience in American Writing," in *Literature and the Sixth Sense* (Boston: Houghton Mifflin, 1970). The essay was originally published in 1940.

57. Philip Rahv, "An Open Secret," in *Literature and the Sixth Sense*, 444–45. The essay was originally published in 1967.

58. The word *plot* here seems to mean simply the movement of feeling and language.

59. Frederick J. Hoffman, Charles Allen, and Carolyn F. Ulrich, *The Little Magazine: A History and a Bibliography* (Princeton, N.J.: Princeton University Press, 1946), 333.

60. "American Qualities," in J. Calder Joseph, *Narration with a Red Piano* (Cincinnati, Ohio: Little Man Press, 1940), 47; hereafter cited in text.

61. Saroyan's contributions to *Hairenik Daily, Hairenik Weekly,* and *Armenian Review* are collected in *My Name Is Saroyan,* ed. James H. Tashjian (New York: Harcourt Brace Jovanovich, 1983).

62. Eugene Jolas, ed., *transition workshop* (New York: Vanguard Press, 1949), 173; hereafter cited in text.

63. Donald McMillan, *Transition: The History of a Literary Era: 1927– 1938* (New York: George Braziller, 1975), 90–101. Jolas in fact began his literary career with the encouragement of Sherwood Anderson, who wrote the introduction to his first book of poems.

64. "Fragment," *transition* 27 (1938): 164.

65. "The Slot Machine (Extracts)," *transition* 27 (1938): 130.

66. Henry Miller, *The Cosmological Eye* (New York: New Directions, 1939), 370; hereafter cited in text.

67. Henry Miller, *Hamlet Letters* (Santa Barbara, Calif.: Capra Press, 1988), 101.

68. Quoted in David Stephen Calonne, *William Saroyan: My Real Name Is Being* (Chapel Hill: University of North Carolina Press, 1983), 158; hereafter cited in text as Calonne.

69. *Sons Come and Go, Mothers Hang in Forever* (New York: McGraw-Hill, 1976), 76.

70. James Laughlin, "Inhale and Exhale: A Letter to Henry Miller," in *William Saroyan: The Man and the Writer Remembered* (Rutherford, N.J.: Fairleigh Dickinson University Press, 1987), 223.

71. William Saroyan, "Saroyan," in *My Name Is Saroyan,* 128.

72. Lawrence Lee and Barry Gifford, *Saroyan: A Biography* (New York: Harper and Row, 1984), 7; hereafter cited in text as Lee and Gifford.

73. *Don't Go Away Mad and Two Other Plays* (London: Faber & Faber, 1951), 127.

74. *Little Children* (New York: Harcourt, Brace, 1937), 6; hereafter cited in text as *Little.*

75. Aram Saroyan, *William Saroyan* (New York: Harcourt Brace Jovanovich, 1983), 33, 35.

76. *The Trouble with Tigers* (New York: Harcourt, Brace, 1938), dedication page; hereafter cited in text as *Trouble.*

77. *"Some Day I'll Be a Millionaire": 34 More Great Stories* (New York: Avon Books, 1944), 12.

78. Stevie Smith, review of *Peace, It's Wonderful, Life and Letters To-Day* 26 (July 1940): 92.

79. *Dear Baby* (New York: Harcourt, Brace, 1944), 92; hereafter cited in text.

80. See, for example, "American Qualities," 46–47.

81. Ernest Hemingway, "Notes on Life and Letters, *Esquire,* May 1935, 21.

82. See, for example, Garig Basmadjian, "Candid Conversation," *Ararat* 25 (Spring 1984): 40; hereafter cited in text.

83. Hemingway's relations with Anderson are documented in Carlos Baker, *Ernest Hemingway: A Life Story* (New York: Charles Scribner's Sons, 1969), passim.

84. *Sweet Drive, Sweet Chariot* (New York: Phaedra, 1966), 50, 49.

85. "A Letter from William Saroyan to James Laughlin," in *Madness in the Family* (New York: New Directions, 1988), 143; hereafter cited in text as *Madness.*

86. "The Barber Whose Uncle Had His Head Bitten off by a Circus Tiger," in *Inhale and Exhale,* 168.

87. Saroyan believed Poe's stories "are, all of them, art stories, and altogether lacking in connexion with real life. . . . Through Poe the short story became excessively formalized, so that for a time it was virtually imprisoned" ("Short Story," 504).

88. *My Name Is Aram* (New York: Harcourt, Brace, 1940), 4; hereafter cited in text as *Aram.* Garoghlanian was Saroyan's maternal grandmother's family name.

89. *Chance Meetings* (New York: W. W. Norton, 1978), 37–38; hereafter cited in text as *Chance.*

90. *A Native American* (San Francisco: George Fields, 1938) included "The Summer of the Beautiful White Horse," "The Journey to Hanford," "One of Our Future Poets, You Might Say," "The Pomegranate Trees," "The Circus," "Locomotive 38, the Ojibway," "A Nice Old Fashioned Romance, with Love Lyrics, and Everything," and "The Fifty Yard Dash." Some 450 copies were published.

91. See the section from Calonne reprinted in part 3 of this volume. Forrest L. Ingram discusses parallels between the two books in *Short Story Cycles of the Twentieth Century* (The Hague: Mouton, 1971). See esp. p. 148.

92. Sherwood Anderson, *Winesburg, Ohio* (New York: Viking Press, 1960), 247.

93. *Saroyan's Fables* (New York: Harcourt, Brace, 1941), 1; hereafter cited in text as *Fables.* The number, of course, does not exist.

94. In my earlier study of Saroyan (*William Saroyan* [Boise, Idaho: Western Writers Series, 1984], 40–43) I discuss *The Human Comedy* as a novel.

95. Although Macauley is an Irish name, Saroyan said that to him the name signified "Mechelian," "Makelian," "Michaelian," or basically anything Armenian (Basmadjian, 43).

96. *The Human Comedy* (New York: Harcourt, Brace, 1943), 150, 154; hereafter cited in text as *Human.*

97. In the revised version this chapter, originally called "It's Your Mis-

fortune and None of My Own," is innocuously retitled "After the Movie" but its final words are changed to read, "pushing down the dark, wet street nearer and nearer to whatever the hell might be next for each of them, God-helping [*sic*]" (William Saroyan, *The Human Comedy*, rev. ed. [New York: Dell Publishing, 1966], 97).

98. Leslie Halliwell, *The Filmgoer's Companion*, 6th ed. (New York: Avon Books, 1978), 323.

99. Neal Gabler discusses Mayer's affection for the movie in *An Empire of Their Own: How the Jews Invented Hollywood* (New York: Crown Publishers, 1988), 388.

100. *Here Comes There Goes You Know Who* (New York: Simon & Schuster, 1961), 140.

101. Saroyan and his wife were remarried in 1951 and divorced again the following year.

102. Ralph Allen, "Pvt. Saroyan and the War," *New York Times Magazine*, 4 June 1944, 46.

103. It is worth noting that under Ottoman rule the Armenians, because they were Christians, were not allowed to be soldiers. Only Moslems were conscripted for the "holy wars," and in fact Armenians were not even allowed to have guns.

104. Irwin Shaw, "Mr. Saroyan's Wartime Comedy," *New York Times Book Review*, 2 June 1946, 1, 16.

105. Edmund Wilson, "Reports on the G.I. by Gertrude Stein and William Saroyan," *New Yorker*, 15 June 1946, 92.

106. Diana Trilling, review of *The Adventures of Wesley Jackson*, *Nation*, 29 June 1946, 788.

107. *The Daring Young Man on the Flying Trapeze* (New York: Yolla Bolly Press, 1984), ix.

108. Philip Rahv, "William Saroyan, a Minority Report," *American Mercury* 57 (September 1943): 372, 375, 374.

109. Philip Rahv, "Paleface and Redskin," in *Literature and the Sixth Sense* (Boston: Houghton, Mifflin 1970), 1–6. The essay first appeared in 1939, midway between Rahv's attack (discussed earlier) on *The Daring Young Man* and his "minority report."

110. Diana Trilling, review of *Dear Baby*, *Nation*, 2 December 1944, 697.

111. Mark Schorer, Technique as Discovery," in *The World We Imagine* (New York: Farrar, Straus, & Giroux, 1968), 23.

112. R. P. Blackmur, "D. H. Lawrence and Expressive Form," in *The Double Agent* (New York: Arrow Editions, 1935), 104, 106; hereafter cited in text.

113. R. P. Blackmur, *The Expense of Greatness* (N.Y.: Arrow Editions, 1940), 190; hereafter cited in text.

114. Saroyan said "The Pheasant Hunter" and "The Third Day after

Christmas" were "tours de force," each written at a single sitting (*Assyrian*, xxi–xxii).

115. Saroyan discussed autobiographical aspects of the story in *Letters from 74 rue Taitbout or Don't Go but if You Must Say Hello to Everybody* (New York: World Publishing, 1969), 28–42; hereafter cited in text as *Letters*.

116. *The Whole Voyald and Other Stories* (Boston: Little, Brown, 1956), 66; hereafter cited in text as *Voyald*.

117. Some, in fact, are addressed to people long since dead.

118. Both *I Used to Believe I Had Forever, Now I'm Not So Sure* and *Letters from 74 rue Taitbout* are included among collections of stories in the lists of Saroyan's publications in, for example, *Days of Life and Death and Escape to the Moon* (New York: Dial, 1970), *Places Where I've Done Time* (New York: Praeger Publishers, 1972), *Sons Come and Go, Mothers Hang in Forever*, and *Chance Meetings*. W.W.

119. The story was first published in the issues of the *Hairenik Daily* published 9 and 10 May 1933. Saroyan did not include it in any of his short story collections, but it is reprinted in *My Name Is Saroyan* (39–44).

120. Saroyan also influenced the filmmaker Robert Altman, whose improvisational, subjective camera work corresponds to Saroyan's expressionist prose. See Patrick McGilligan, "Mr. Saroyan's Thoroughly American Movie," in *The American Film and the Movies*, ed. Gerald Peary and Roger Shattzkin (New York: Ungar, 1978), 159.

121. John Clellon Holmes, "The Great Rememberer," in *Representative Men: The Biographical Essays* (Fayetteville: University of Arkansas Press, 1988), 129.

122. Ted Berrigan, "Jack Kerouac," in *On the Road: Text and Criticism*, ed. Scott Donaldson (New York: Viking Penguin, 1979), 555. Aram Saroyan accompanied Berrigan to the interview "because Ted, knowing that Kerouac had loved my father's work, thought [Kerouac] might be more responsive with me in tow" (Aram Saroyan, "My Sixties," *American Poetry Review* 19 [January/February 1990]: 32).

123. Jack Kerouac, *Heaven and Other Poems* (Bolinas, Calif.: Grey Fox Press, 1977), 51. Kerouac also acknowledged Saroyan's influence in, among other works, *Vanity of Dulvoz* (New York: Coward, McCann, 1968), 99.

124. Warren French (*Jack Kerouac* [Boston: Twayne Publishers, 1986], 29) suggests that the character of Mickey in this novel "is strongly reminiscent of the sentimental characters in William Saroyan's *The Human Comedy.*"

125. Allen Ginsberg, *Composed on the Tongue* (Bolinas, Calif.: Grey Fox Press, 1980), 41.

126. Jack Kerouac, "Essentials of Spontaneous Prose," in *On the Road: Text and Criticism*, 531.

127. Warren Tallman, "Kerouac's Sound," in *On the Road: Text and Criticism*, 521–22.

128. George Wickes, ed., *Lawrence Durrell and Henry Miller: A Private Correspondence* (New York: E. P. Dutton, 1963), 348.

129. Jack Kerouac, *On the Road: Text and Criticism*, 254.

130. Jack Kerouac, *Visions of Cody* (New York: McGraw-Hill, 1972), 398.

131. Lawrence Lipton, *The Holy Barbarians* (New York: Grove Press, 1959), 232.

132. Introduction to David Kherdian *Six Poets of the San Francisco Poetry Renaissance*, (Fresno, Calif.: Giligia Press, 1967), xii–xiii.

133. Elizabeth Bowen, "In Spite of the Words," *New Republic*, 9 March 1953, 18.

Part 2

THE WRITER

Introduction

Asked by his friends Whit and Hallie Burnett, "What is the form of your most characteristic literary work?" Saroyan replied, "The truest form is myself."[1] In his prefaces, essays, and memoirs Saroyan returned repeatedly to his belief that the literary work was, at least for him, not a tooled, objective creation but the intimate and immediate expression of what he most essentially was. That identity in turn was specifically Armenian.

The following selections suggest ways in which Saroyan viewed his work and the importance of his Armenian heritage to it. The passages reprinted from Zori Balayan's interview, "Arguments for Soviet Power . . . ," deal with Saroyan's aesthetic theories and sense of ethnic identity. (*Varpet*, the Armenian word with which Balayan addresses Saroyan, means "Master.")

Saroyan's preface to the first edition of *The Daring Young Man on the Flying Trapeze* is the earliest of many pieces summarizing the way he thought writing should be done, which essentially meant doing whatever you were doing, whatever way you felt you should. The importance to Saroyan of his ethnic identity is suggested in the passage from his introduction to an anthology entitled *Hairenik: 1934–1939*. The *Hairenik Weekly* was an Armenian publication to which Saroyan frequently contributed, and the anthology collected poems, stories, and translations that had been published there. Saroyan believed the anthology was the first of its kind in America, and he hoped there would soon be similar books by other "racial minorities": "out of this kind of healthy racial consciousness in the second-and-third-generation American," he said, "is likely to appear the most satisfactory kind of new American."[2]

"Antranik of Armenia," discussed in Part 1 of this volume, is one of Saroyan's most famous works. It is his strongest and most fully developed expression of the Armenian character and sensibility that informed his writing.

The final selection is from letters written by Isabella L. Bird in 1890 and collected in her *Journeys in Persia and Kurdistan* the following year.

Her British and missionary sympathies are clear, but she is otherwise an objective, reliable guide to the Ottoman provinces in the final years of the empire. She admired the Kurds in many ways (indeed, for her "Armenia" was "Kurdistan"), but she knew they could be brutal with Christians, and she did not understate the terror that was a simple fact of life for the Armenians.

The Bitlis she describes is the city from which the Saroyans, beginning in 1893, fled. More than a dozen years passed before the last of the family reached America, where Saroyan was born in 1908. Although he did not see the city until 1964, it was imaginatively of great importance to him. In 1975 he wrote a play titled *Bitlis*, and in it the character Saroyan based on himself says it was essential for him to see the place at last. His companion understands—in a way, the city must have been so important for Saroyan that it was almost as if he had always lived there. But there were no Saroyans left in the city, and there were only ruins where their homes had stood.

Notes

1. Whit Burnett and Hallie Burnett, *The Modern Short Story in the Making* (New York: Hawthorn Books, 1964), 224.

2. William Saroyan, introduction to *Hairenik: 1934–1939*, ed. Reuben Darbinian (Boston: Hairenik Press, 1939), xv.

Interview with William Saroyan

Zori Balayan

Balayan: Your so-called autobiographicism? Do you consider that fair?

Saroyan: In accusing me of this, my critics never suspected that they were deliberately or by chance describing precisely what I am as a writer. In the final count, a novel *is* the novelist and a story *is* the story-teller. We recognise a writer not only by his style but by the depth of the author's feelings as a person, as an individual. I, for example, will never believe that all the excruciating spiritual agony that we perceive in Dostoevsky's heroes could have been thought up sitting at one's desk, so to speak. My eye was once caught by a title: it was either *The Story of What I Have Experienced* or perhaps *The Story of What I Lived Through*. I felt that one should not give one's writings such titles because writers always write about what they have experienced or lived through. That is why I don't accept the term "autobiographicism." Hemingway's personal life is all in his books. I greatly love and value Thomas Wolfe and I remember that I even rejoiced when he, too, was accused of the same notorious "ism."

Balayan: You told me, Varpet, that you are by nature a pagan, that you have many gods who protect you as you write. Please name some of them.

Saroyan: Truth, sincerity, irony. . . .

Balayan: You were given the New York Critics' Prize for your book *The Time of Your Life*. What is your attitude to criticism nowadays?

Saroyan: Personally, I cannot only make do without criticism, I can do this quite happily. I think that in a certain sense literature, too, can live without it, something which cannot be said about criticism since it could hardly exist without literature. Back in the distant past when

Excerpted from "Arguments for Soviet Power . . . ," *Soviet Literature* 12, no. 367 (1977): 160–66. © 1977 by *Soviet Literature*. Reprinted by permission.

the *Iliad* and the *Odyssey* were being written, there was no official criticism and it didn't matter: it was not because of that, I think, that
Homer went blind in his old age. As for myself, I must admit that I
like it when I'm praised but that I don't worry too much when I'm
hammered. In this as in many other things, I feel endlessly close to
and in sympathy with the great Chekhov from whom I learned—how
shall I put it?—culture, perhaps. He believed that one should not respond to criticism. That is a wonderful principle. Not everyone has
enough courage and dignity not to react to criticism. If you think about
it, the critic is either right or wrong. If he is right, then it's stupid to
answer him and if he is wrong, then it is even more senseless to tangle
with him since in that event he must be either unintelligent or dishonest. A feeling, though, prompts me to say that criticism is an independ-
ent literary genre. Or at least, I think, that is what it should be. . . .

Balayan: Do you like poetry?

Saroyan: I was asked the same question by Grant Matevosyan. He
asked it and immediately himself began to answer it for me. He said
that I am a prose-writing poet. I realise that what he is referring to is a
certain lyricism in my writings. However, I do also write poetry. I began my writing career with poetry. And I still write the occasional
poem. But I never publish them. Let that be done for me after my
death. The reason I write poems is, I suppose, because I need them.
And perhaps I need them in order always to feel the power of the *mot
juste*, the power of brevity, contempt for long-windedness and, of
course, to "feel" the imagery. In my opinion, it is images and imagery
that at the final count distinguish the poet from the non-poet, the artist
from the artisan. And the whole thing is that a person who never writes
any poetry can be a poet and an artist. Take, for example, Grigor Gurzadyan. I am told that he built an instrument which was put into space.
I would have felt robbed had I not had a meeting with Gurzadyan. I
am not very clear what it is he works on. I saw some English translations of his monographs on his desk: I read the titles and couldn't understand a thing. The object of my research is the human soul while
he studies outer space and the stars. He could spend a hundred years
explaining to me, what he does and I would still not be able to understand him. But suddenly he began to use imagery. And I understood
that our capacity for carrying out observations of the Galaxy from the
Earth has been exhausted. What we have achieved is that we now have
in our hands a piece of the tail of an immense and unknown animal

and from this piece we are trying to gather an impression of the animal itself. By taking his telescope out into space, the scientist's ability to observe is increased many times over.

And how wonderfully Grigor spoke about his stars! How his eyes shone! He spoke and I couldn't understand a thing. He talked about the life and death of stars—and again I understood nothing. I only know about the life and death of men, trees, and lakes. And he, as if reading my thoughts, began talking about the apple tree. I will never in my life forget Gurzadyan's tree. I can even see a real, utterly real, apple tree growing out there, in space. This nice man of whom I became very fond spoke about how we have different ideas about stars not because they are so different one from another but because we see them at different times in their lives. And, evidently noticing that I was again toiling and suffering from my own thickheadedness, he said that I should imagine we were looking at a tree in winter. It is dried out and as if dead. In spring, however, it is quite another matter: it seems somehow to sing and is covered with a pink and white cloud of blooms. It is yet another tree in late summer or at the beginning of autumn. There is already something Biblical about it. Fruits hang from it like toys from a Christmas tree. Of course, if a person were to see these three so different apple trees at the same time, he would hardly think that it was one and the same tree. Apple trees and stars. . . . It's superb! It's simply a miracle and it's something I must write about. I am a person who is not only far from politics but also from science. I nevertheless take my hat off to scientists and especially to those who in their souls are poets. If a scientist is a poet in his soul, it means that he will create only good.

To our good fortune, Gurzadyan is furthermore also an artist. Whenever I use this word I now always recall Minas Avetisyan. He is a great artist. And that he should have departed from us so early is a great tragedy for modern art. Minas is also a poet. I love poets, I love poetry. . . .

Balayan: Varpet, you've written over 2,000 stories, not counting a vast number of novels and plays. . . .

Saroyan: Since we have agreed that this is not simply a conversation in a car as it bumps merrily down the road to Garni but a real interview, this means that you are now going to ask me what I am working on and what plans I have for the future. I won't tell you. This is not because it's a secret and neither is it a matter of superstition. It's simply that I am always working, always writing. I am a writer. I write about people. In order to tell you what I am now working on, I would have to give you a résumé of the plot. And a plot is nothing more than an anecdote.

I would prefer your readers to learn that William Saroyan on a beautiful misty day set off specially to see an ancient pagan place of worship. Everyone will understand that one can't visit Armenia without going to see Garni. I have in fact seen Garni before. On the way from Leningrad to Yerevan, Razmik Davoyan and Levon Mkrtchyan showed me a photograph of Garni in *Pravda*. Incidentally, let me add something to what I have just said. The restoration of this ancient pagan temple, this priceless monument of world culture, is also an argument for Soviet power. . . .

Balayan: One of our literary magazines had a section for writers called "How Do You Write?" What would you answer to such a question?

Saroyan: I don't know. Could one really ask a baker, for example, "How do you bake bread?" And if you did ask, do you really think he would be able to describe to you how he bakes bread? I don't know how I write. I can only say one thing: I write every day. Never and nowhere am I without my typewriter. Every day—that is very important. Because if you write every day, you can't help but say something valuable at least once a year.

Balayan: It's not polite to remind guests of their departure date. I would therefore like to ask you when you next intend to come to the Soviet Union?

Saroyan: I am not at all a guest here. Each time I come here, it is to my home, to my fellow-countrymen. I may come here in a year's time.

Balayan: In a year's time you will be 70. . . .

Saroyan: In a year's time, it will be a hundred and fifty years since Eastern Armenia joined Russia. I would like to celebrate this great holiday together with my fellow-countrymen. I am not blind and I can see what has become of my country. I know what it was once like. William Saroyan was born on alien soil. I want people to be born on the land of their forebears.

Preface to The Daring Young Man on the Flying Trapeze and Other Stories

I am writing this preface to the first edition so that in the event that this book is issued in a second edition I will be able to write a preface to the second edition, explaining what I said in the preface to the first edition and adding a few remarks about what I have been doing in the meantime, and so on.

In the event that the book reaches a third edition, it is my plan to write a preface to the third edition, covering all that I said in the prefaces to the first and second editions, and it is my plan to go on writing prefaces for new editions of this book until I die. After that I hope there will be children and grandchildren to keep up the good work.

In this early preface, when I have no idea how many copies of the book are going to be sold, the only thing I can do is talk about how I came to write these stories.

Years ago when I was getting a thorough grammar-school education in my home town I found out that stories were something very odd that some sort of men had been turning out (for some odd reason) for hundreds of years, and that there were rules governing the writing of stories.

I immediately began to study all the classic rules, including Ring Lardner's, and in the end I discovered that the rules were wrong.

The trouble was, they had been leaving me out, and as far as I could tell I was the most important element in the matter, so I made some new rules.

I wrote rule Number One when I was eleven and had just been sent home from the fourth grade for having talked out of turn and meant it.

Do not pay any attention to the rules other people make, I wrote.

From William Saroyan, *The Daring Young Man on the Flying Trapeze and Other Stories* (New York: Random House, 1934), 9–13. Reprinted by permission of the William Saroyan Foundation.

They make them for their own protection, and to hell with them. (I was pretty sore that day.)

Several months later I discovered rule Number Two, which caused a sensation. At any rate, it was a sensation with me. This rule was: Forget Edgar Allan Poe and O. Henry and write the kind of stories you feel like writing. Forget everybody who ever wrote anything.

Since that time I have added four other rules and I have found this number to be enough. Sometimes I do not have to bother about rules at all, and I just sit down and write. Now and then I stand and write.

My third rule was: Learn to typewrite, so you can turn out stories as fast as Zane Grey.

It is one of my best rules.

But rules without a system are, as every good writer will tell you, utterly inadequate. You can leave out "utterly" and the sentence will mean the same thing, but it is always nicer to throw in an "utterly" whenever possible. All successful writers believe that one word by it-self hasn't enough meaning and that it is best to emphasize the meaning of one word with the help of another. Some writers will go so far as to help an innocent word with as many as four and five other words, and at times they will kill an innocent word by charity and it will take years and years for some ignorant writer who doesn't know adjectives at all to resurrect the word that was killed by kindness.

Anyway, these stories are the result of a method of composition.

I call it the Festival or Fascist method of composition, and it works this way:

Someone who isn't a writer begins to want to be a writer and he keeps on wanting to be one for ten years, and by that time he has convinced all his relatives and friends and even himself that he *is* a writer, but he hasn't written a thing and he is no longer a boy, so he is getting worried. All he needs now is a system. Some authorities claim there are as many as fifteen systems, but actually there are only two: (1) you can decide to write like Anatole France or Alexandre Dumas or somebody else, or (2) you can decide to forget that you are a writer at all and you can decide to sit down at your typewriter and put words on paper, one at a time, in the best fashion you know how—which brings me to the matter of style.

The matter of style is one that always excites controversy, but to me it is as simple as A B C, if not simpler.

A writer can have, ultimately, one of two styles: he can write in a manner that implies that death is inevitable, or he can write in a manner that implies that death is *not* inevitable. Every style ever employed by a writer has been influenced by one or another of these attitudes toward death.

If you write as if you believe that ultimately you and everyone else alive will be dead, there is a chance that you will write in a pretty earnest style. Otherwise you are apt to be either pompous or soft. On the other hand, in order not to be a fool, you must believe that as much as death is inevitable life is inevitable. That is, the earth is inevitable, and people and other living things on it are inevitable, but that no man can remain on the earth very long. You do not have to be melodramatically tragic about this. As a matter of fact, you can be as amusing as you like about it. It is really one of the basically humorous things, and it has all sorts of possibilities for laughter. If you will remember that living people are as good as dead, you will be able to perceive much that is very funny in their conduct that you perhaps might never have thought of perceiving if you did not believe that they were as good as dead.

The most solid advice, though, for a writer is this, I think: Try to learn to breathe deeply, really to taste food when you eat, and when you sleep, really to sleep. Try as much as possible to be wholly alive, with all your might, and when you laugh, laugh like hell, and when you get angry, get good and angry. Try to be alive. You will be dead soon enough.

From the Introduction to
Hairenik: 1934–1939

The aesthetic by itself is neither a foolish nor a special thing; it simply tends to grow foolish when men seek to make it uncommon or special. I say this by way of preparing the reader for the simple truth I wish him to consider carefully; namely, that living and writing are the same thing, and that at its best reading also is living. Living is spontaneous and immediate, with conditioning from the past and the future; writing is spontaneous and immediate and at the same time a kind of living which is extra; and still at the same time writing is the immortality of the writer and the immortality of the reader.

From the isolation, emphasis, and clarification of human experience in writing, living has its greatest meaning and its best chance to survive nobly.

It is important, I am trying to say, for writing to continue, for through its continuance is the continuance of living itself. This is a thing I know without a question of doubt.

The writing I am speaking of is not, however, the inconsequential thing called writing which has come to be in America because of writing's foolish entanglement in the multitude of material things which nullify it at its source: within the man himself. I have no quarrel with commercial writing. I have no quarrel with writers who write for money, as merchants buy and sell for money. I am simply making a necessary distinction.

I speak here of the innocent and inevitable writing which, good or bad, is written out of the impulse in men to truly be alive, and to achieve the personal maximum from the experience of mortality.

The important thing for this writing is that it shall be written, and printed. It is no matter if it is not read, or if it is read and not understood and appreciated, or if it is read and disliked. Allowing the im-

Excerpted from *Hairenik: 1934–1939*, ed. Reuben Darbinian (Boston: Hairenik Press, 1939), xi–xii. Reprinted by permission of the Hairenik Association, Inc.

pulse to be fulfilled is the important thing, not the writing itself. At the beginning this writing is likely to be artless, formless, ineffective, unimportant, and one or another of the undesired things in living. Even this does not matter. The important thing, I repeat, is that the true beginning be made. A right beginning may be followed by errors for a while, but a wrong beginning will always bring about waste.

The urgent thing for writing is that it shall not be kept by any force from reaching the reality of word and print, that wherever and whenever its necessity appears in a man, he will find it possible and desirable to accept the necessity, and pleasant and satisfying to fulfill it, and get the writing on paper. The impulse to write is the impulse to live, and it is important for any who wish to live, to do so. That is all it comes to.

"Antranik of Armenia"

I didn't learn to speak Armenian until my grandmother came to our house and every morning sang about Antranik the soldier until I knew he was an Armenian, a mountain peasant on a black horse who with only a handful of men was fighting the enemy. That was in 1915, the year of physical pain and spiritual disintegration for the people of my country, and the people of the world, but I was seven and I didn't know. From my own meaningless grief I could imagine something was wrong in the world, but I didn't know what. My grandmother sang in a way that made me begin to find out, singing mournfully and with great anger, in a strong voice, while she worked in the house. I picked up the language in no time because it was in me in the first place and all I needed to do was fit the words to the remembrance. I was an Armenian. God damn the bastards who were making the trouble. (That is the way it is when you are an Armenian, and it is wrong. There are no bastards. The bitter feeling of the Armenian is also the bitter feeling of the Turk. It is all absurd, but I did not know. I did not know the Turk is a simple, amiable, helpless man who does what he is forced to do. I did not know that hating him was the same as hating the Armenian since they were the same. My grandmother didn't know either, and still does not know. I know now, but I don't know what good it is going to do me because there is still idiocy in the world and by idiocy I mean everything lousy, like ignorance and, what is still worse, willful blindness. Everybody in the world knows there is no such thing as nationality, but look at them. Look at Germany, Italy, France, England. Look at Russia even. Look at Poland. Just look at all the crazy maniacs. I can't figure out why they won't open their eyes and see that it is all idiocy. I can't figure out why they won't learn to use their strength for life instead of death, but it looks as if they won't. My grandmother is too old to learn, but how about all the people in the world who were born less than thirty years ago? How about all those

From *Inhale and Exhale* (New York: Random House, 1936), William Saroyan, 257–65. Reprinted by permission of the William Saroyan Foundation.

people? Are they too young to learn? Or is it proper to work only for death?)

In 1915 General Antranik was part of the cause of the trouble in the world, but it wasn't his fault. There was no other way out for him and he was doing only what he had to do. The Turks were killing Armenians and General Antranik and his soldiers were killing Turks. He was killing fine, simple, amiable Turks, but he wasn't destroying any real criminal because every real criminal was far from the scene of fighting. An eye for an eye, but always the wrong eye. And my grandmother prayed for the triumph and safety of General Antranik, although she knew Turks were good people. She herself said they were.

General Antranik had the same job in Armenia and Turkey that Lawrence of Arabia had in Arabia: to harass the Turkish Army and keep it from being a menace to the armies of Italy and France and England. General Antranik was a simple Armenian peasant who believed the governments of England and France and Italy when these governments told him his people would be given their freedom for making trouble for the Turkish Army. He was not an adventurous and restless English writer who was trying to come to terms with himself as to what was valid in the world for him, and unlike Lawrence of Arabia General Antranik did not know that what he was doing was stupid and futile because after the trouble the governments of England and France and Italy would betray him. He did not know a strong government needs and seeks the friendship of another strong government, and after the war there was nothing in the world for him or the people of Armenia. The strong governments talked about doing something for Armenia, but they never did anything. And the war was over and General Antranik was only a soldier, not a soldier and a diplomat and a writer. He was only an Armenian. He didn't fight the Turkish Army because it would give him something to write about. He didn't write two words about the whole war. He fought the Turkish Army because he was an Armenian. When the war ended and the fine diplomatic negotiating began General Antranik was lost. The Turkish government looked upon him as a criminal and offered a large sum of money for his capture, dead or alive. General Antranik escaped to Bulgaria, but Turkish patriots followed him to Bulgaria, so he came to America.

General Antranik came to my home town. It looked as if all the Armenians in California were at the Southern Pacific depot the day he arrived. I climbed a telephone pole and saw him when he got off the train. He was a man of about fifty in a neat American suit of clothes.

He was a little under six feet tall, very solid and very strong. He had an old-style Armenian moustache that was white. The expression of his face was both ferocious and kindly. The people swallowed him up and a committee got him into a great big Cadillac and drove away with him.

I got down from the telephone pole and ran all the way to my uncle's office. That was in 1919 or 1920, and I was eleven or twelve. Maybe it was a year or two later. It doesn't make any difference. Anyway, I was working in my uncle's office as office boy. All I used to do was go out and get him a cold watermelon once in a while which he used to cut in the office, right on his desk. He used to eat the big half and I used to eat the little half. If a client came to see him while he was eating watermelon, I would tell the client my uncle was very busy and ask him to wait in the reception room or come back in an hour. Those were the days for me and my uncle. He was a lawyer with a good practice and I was his nephew, his sister's son, as well as a reader of books. We used to talk in Armenian and English and spit the seeds into the cuspidor.

My uncle was sitting at his desk, all excited, smoking a cigarette.

Did you see Antranik? he said in Armenian.

In Armenian we never called him General Antranik, only in English.

I saw him, I said.

My uncle was very excited. Here, he said. Here's a quarter. Go and get a big cold watermelon.

When I came back with the watermelon there were four men in the office, the editor of the *Asbarez*, another lawyer, and two clients, farmers. They were all smoking cigarettes and talking about Antranik. My uncle gave me a dollar and told me to go and get as many more watermelons as I could carry. I came back with a big watermelon under each arm and my uncle cut each melon in half and each of us had half a melon to eat. There were only two big spoons and one butter knife, so the two farmers ate with their fingers, and so did I.

My uncle represented one of the farmers, and the other lawyer represented the other. My uncle's client said he had loaned two hundred dollars to the other farmer three years ago but had neglected to get a note, and the other farmer said he had never borrowed a penny from anybody. That was the argument, but nobody was bothering about it now. We were all eating watermelon and being happy about Antranik. At last the other attorney said, About this little matter?

My uncle squirted some watermelon seeds from his mouth into the cuspidor and turned to the other lawyer's client.

Did Hovsep lend you two hundred dollars three years ago? he said.

Yes, that is true, said the other farmer.

He dug out a big chunk of the heart of the watermelon with his fingers and pushed it into his mouth.

But yesterday, said the other lawyer, you told me he didn't lend you a penny.

That was yesterday, said the farmer. Today I saw Antranik. I have no money now, but I will pay him just as soon as I sell my crop.

Brother, said the farmer named Hovsep to the other farmer, that's all I wanted to know. I loaned you two hundred dollars because you needed the money, and I wanted you to pay me so people wouldn't laugh at me for being a fool. Now it is different. I don't want you to pay me. It is a gift to you. I don't need the money.

No, brother, said the other farmer, a debt is a debt. I insist upon paying.

My uncle swallowed watermelon, listening to the two farmers.

I don't want the money, said the farmer named Hovsep.

I borrowed two hundred dollars from you, didn't I? said the other farmer.

Yes.

Then I must pay you back.

No, brother, I will not accept the money.

But you must.

No.

The other farmer turned to his lawyer bitterly. Can we take the case to court and make him take the money? he said.

The other lawyer looked at my uncle whose mouth was full of watermelon. He looked at my uncle in a way that was altogether comical and Armenian, meaning, Well, what the hell do you call this? and my uncle almost choked with laughter and watermelon and seeds.

Then all of us busted out laughing, even the two farmers.

Countrymen, said my uncle. Go home. Forget this unimportant matter. This is a great day for us. Our hero Antranik has come to us from Hairenik, our native land. Go home and be happy.

The two farmers went away, talking together about the great event.

Every Armenian in California was happy about the arrival of Antranik from the old country.

One day six or seven months later Antranik came to my uncle's office when I was there. I knew he had visited my uncle many times while I was away from the office, in school, but this was the first time I had seen him so closely, he himself, the man, our great national hero General Antranik, in the very room where I sat with my uncle. I felt very angry and sad because I could see how bewildered and bitter and disappointed he was. Where was the glorious new Armenia he had dreamed of winning for his people? Where was the magnificent resurrection of the ancient race?

He came into the office quietly, almost shyly, as only a great man can be quiet and shy, and my uncle jumped up from his desk, loving him more than he loved any other man in the world, and through him loving the lost nation, the multitude dead, and the multitude living in every alien corner of the world. And I with my uncle, jumping up and loving him the same way, but him only, Antranik, the great man fallen to nothing, the soldier helpless in a world now full of cheap and false peace, he himself betrayed and his people betrayed, and Armenia only a memory.

He talked quietly for about an hour and then went away, and when I looked at my uncle I saw that tears were in his eyes and his mouth was twisting with agony like the mouth of a small boy who is in great pain but will not let himself cry.

That was what came of our little part in the bad business of 1915, and it will be the same with other nations, great and small, for many years to come because that way is the bad way, the wasteful way, and even if your nation is strong enough to win the war, death of one sort or another is the only ultimate consequence, death, not life, is the only end, and it is always people, not nations, because it is all one nation, the living, so why won't they change the way? Why do they want to go on fooling themselves? They know there are a lot of finer ways to be strong than to be strong in numbers, in war, so why don't they cut it out? What do they want to do to all the fine, amiable, simple people of every nation in the world? The Turk is the brother of the Armenian and they know it. The German and the Frenchman, the Russian and the Pole, the Japanese and the Chinese. They are all brothers. They are all small tragic entities of mortality. Why do they want them to kill one another? What good does it do anybody?

I like the swell exhilaration that comes from having one's body and mind in opposition to some strong force, but why should that force be one's own brothers instead of something less subject to the agonies of mortality? Why can't the God damn war be a nobler kind of war? Is every noble problem of man solved? Is there nothing more to do but kill? Everybody knows there are other things to do, so why won't they cut out the monkey business?

The governments of strong nations betrayed Antranik and Armenia after the war, but the soldiers of Armenia refused to betray themselves. It was no joke with them. It would be better to be dead, they said, than to be betrayed by their own intelligence into new submission. To fight was to be impractical, but not to fight was to be racially nullified. They knew it would be suicide because they had no friend in the world. The governments of strong nations were busy with complex diplomatic problems of their own. Their war was ended and the time had come for conversation. For the soldiers of Armenia the time had come for death or great good fortune, and the Armenian is too wise to believe in great good fortune.

These were the Nationalists, the *Tashnaks*, and they fought for Armenia, for the nation Armenia, because it was the only way they knew how to fight for life and dignity and race. The world had no other way. It was with guns only. The diplomats had no time for Armenia. It was the bad way, the God damn lousy way, but these men were great men and they did what they had to do, and any Armenian who despises these men is either ignorant or a traitor to his race. These men were dead wrong. I know they were dead wrong, but it was the only way. Well, they won the war. (No war is ever won: that is a technical term, used solely to save space and time.) Somehow or other the whole race was not annihilated. The people of Armenia were cold and hungry and ill, but these soldiers won their war and Armenia was a nation with a government, a political party, the *Tashnaks*. (That is so sad, that is so pathetic when you think of the thousands who were killed, but I honor the soldiers, those who died and those who still live. These I honor and love, and all who compromised I only love.) It was a ghastly mistake, but it was a noble mistake, and Armenia was Armenia. It was a very small nation of course, a very unimportant nation, surrounded on all sides by enemies, but for two years Armenia was Armenia, and the capital was Erivan. For the first time in thousands of years Armenia was Armenia.

I know how silly it is to be proud, but I cannot help it, I am proud.

The war was with the Turks of course. The other enemies were less active than the Turks, but watchful. When the time came one of these, in the name of love, not hate, accomplished in no time at all what the

Turks, who were more honest, whose hatred was unconcealed, could not accomplish in hundreds of years. These were the Russians. The new ones. They were actually the old ones, but they had a new theory and they said their idea was brotherhood on earth. They made a brother of Armenia at the point of a gun, but even so, if brotherhood was really their idea, that's all right. They killed all the leaders of the Armenian soldiers, but nobody will hold that against them either. Very few of the Armenians of Armenia wanted to be brothers to the new Russians, but each of them was hungry and weary of the war and consequently the revolt against the new enemy was brief and tragic. It ended in no time at all. It looked like the world simply wouldn't let the Armenians have their own country, even after thousands of years, even after more than half of the Armenians of Asia Minor had been killed. They just didn't want the Armenians to have their nation. So it turned out that the leaders of the Armenian soldiers were criminals, so they were shot. That's all. The Russian brothers just shot them. Then they told the Armenians not to be afraid, the Turks wouldn't bother them any more. The brotherly Russian soldiers marched through the streets of the cities of Armenia and told everybody not to be afraid. Every soldier had a gun. There was a feeling of great brotherliness in Armenia.

Away out in California I sat in my uncle's office. To hell with it, I said. It's all over. We can begin to forget Armenia now. Antranik is dead. The nation is lost. The strong nations of the world are jumping with new problems. To hell with the whole God damn mess, I said. I'm no Armenian. I'm an American.

Well, the truth is I am both and neither. I love Armenia and I love America and I belong to both, but I am only this: an inhabitant of the earth, and so are you, whoever you are.

I tried to forget Armenia but I couldn't do it. My birthplace was California, but I couldn't forget Armenia, so what is one's country? Is it land of the earth, in a specific place? Rivers there? Lakes? The sky there? The way the moon comes up there? And the sun? Is one's country the trees, the vineyards, the grass, the birds, the rocks, the hills and mountains and valleys? Is it the temperature of the place in spring and summer and winter? Is it the animal rhythm of the living there? The huts and houses, the streets of cities, the tables and chairs, and the drinking of tea and talking? Is it the peach ripening in summer heat on the bough? Is it the dead in the earth there? The unborn of love beginning? Is it the sound of the spoken language in all the places of that country under the sky? The printed word of that language? The picture painted there? The song of that throat and heart? That dance? Is one's country their prayers of thanks for air and water and earth and fire and life? Is it their eyes? Their lips smiling? The grief?

Well, I do not know for sure, but I know it is all these things as remembrance in the blood. It is all these things within one's self, because I have been there, I have been to Armenia and I have seen with my own eyes, and I know. I have been to the place. Armenia. There is no nation there, but that is all the better. But I have been to that place, and I know this: that there is no nation in the world, no England and France and Italy, and no nation whatsoever. And I know that each who lives upon the earth is no more than a tragic entity of mortality, let him be king or beggar. I would like to see them awaken to this truth and stop killing one another because I believe there are other and finer ways to be great and brave and exhilarated. I believe there are ways whose ends are life instead of death. What difference does it make what the nation is or what political theory governs it? Does that in any way decrease for its subjects the pain and sorrow of mortality? Or in any way increase the strength and delight?

I went to see. To find out. To breathe that air. To be in that place.

The grapes of the Armenian vineyards were not yet ripe, but there were fresh green leaves, and the vines were exactly like the vines of California, and the faces of the Armenians of Armenia were exactly like the faces of the Armenians of California. The rivers Arax and Kura moved slowly through the fertile earth of Armenia in the same way that the rivers Kings and San Joaquin moved through the valley of my birthplace. And the sun was warm and kindly, no less than the sun of California.

And it was nowhere and everywhere. It was different and exactly the same, word for word, pebble for pebble, leaf for leaf, eye for eye and tooth for tooth. It was neither Armenia nor Russia. It was people alive in that place, and not people only, but all things alive there, animate and inanimate: the vines, the trees, the rocks, the rivers, the streets, the buildings, the whole place, urban and rural, nowhere and everywhere. The earth again. And it was sad. The automobile bounced over the dirt road to the ancient Armenian church at Aitchmiadzin, and the peasants, men and women and children, stood in bare feet on the ancient stone floor, looking up at the cross, bowing their heads, and believing. And the Armenian students of Marx laughed humbly and a little shamefully at the innocent unwisdom and foolish faith of their brothers. And the sadness of Armenia, my country, was so great in me that, sitting in the automobile, returning to Erivan, the only thing I could remember about Armenia was the quiet way General Antranik talked with my uncle many years ago and the tears in my uncle's eyes when he was gone, and the painful way my uncle's lips were twisting.

From Journeys in Persia and Kurdistan

Isabella L. Bird

Bitlis, November 12 [1890]—This is the most romantically-situated city that I have seen in Western Asia. The dreamy impressions of height and depth received on the night of my arrival were more than realized the following morning. Even to the traveller arriving by daylight Bitlis must come as a great surprise, for it is situated in a hole upon which the upper valley descends with a sudden dip. The Bitlis-chai or Eastern Tigris passes through it in a series of raging cataracts, and is joined in the middle of the town by another torrent tumbling down another wild valley, and from this meeting of the waters massive stone houses rise one above another singly, and in groups and terraces, producing a singularly striking effect. Five valleys appear to unite in Bitlis and to radiate from a lofty platform of rock supported on precipices, the irregular outlines of which are emphasized by walls and massive square and circular towers, the gigantic ruins of Bitlis Castle.

The massiveness of the houses is remarkable, and their courtyards and gardens are enclosed by strong walls. Every gate is strengthened and studded with iron, every window is heavily barred, all are at a considerable height, and every house looks as if it could stand a siege. There is no room to spare; the dwellings are piled tier above tier, and the flagged footways in front of them hang on the edges of precipices. Twenty picturesque stone bridges, each one of a single arch, span the Tigris and the torrents which unite with it. There are ancient ruins scattered through the town. It claims immense antiquity, and its inhabitants ascribe its castle and some of its bridges to Alexander the Great, but antiquarians attribute the former either to the Saracens or to the days when an ancient Armenian city called Paghesh occupied the site

Excerpted from Isabella L. Bird, *Journeys in Persia and Kurdistan*, vol. 2 (London: John Murray, 1891), 350–52, 354–55.

of the present Bitlis. It seems like the end of the world, though through the deep chasms below it, through which the Tigris descends with great rapidity to the plains, lies the highway to Diabekir. Suggestions of the ancient world abound. The lofty summits towering above the basin in which this extraordinary city lies are the termination of the Taurus chain, the Niphates of the ancients, on the highest peak of which Milton localised the descent of Satan.

Remote as Bitlis seems and is, its markets are among the busiest in Turkey, and its caravan traffic is enormous for seven or eight months of the year. Its altitude is only 4700 feet, and the mercury in winter rarely falls to zero, but the snowfall is tremendous, and on the Rahwan Plain snow frequently lies up to the top of the telegraph poles, isolating the town and shutting up animals in their stables and human beings in their houses for weeks, and occasionally months, at a time. . . .

Bitlis is one of the roughest and most fanatical and turbulent of Turkish cities, but the present Governor, Raouf Pasha, is a man of energy, and has reduced the town and neighbourhood to some degree of order. Considerable bodies of troops have been brought in, and the garrison consists of 2500 men. These soldiers are thoroughly well clothed and equipped, and look remarkably clean in dress and person. They are cheery, soldierly-looking men, and their presence gives a little confidence to the Christians.

The population of Bitlis is estimated at 30,000, of which number over 20,000 are Kurds. Both men and women are very handsome, and the striking Kurdish costume gives a great brilliancy and picturesqueness to this remarkable city. . . .

The population is by far the wildest that I have seen in any Asiatic city, and is evidently only restrained from violence by the large garrison. It is not safe for the ladies of this mission to descend into the Moslem part of the city, and in a residence of more than twenty years they have never even passed through the bazaars. The missionaries occupy a restricted and uncertain position, and the Armenian Christians are subject to great deprivations and restraints, and are distrusted by the Government. Of late they have been much harassed by the search for arms, and Christian gunsmiths have been arrested. Even their funeral ceremonies are not exempt from the presence of the police, who profess to believe that firearms are either carried in the place of a corpse or are concealed along with it. Placed in the midst of a preponderating and fully-armed Kurdish population, capable at any moment of being excited to frenzy against their faith, they live in expectation of a massacre, should certain events take place which are regarded as probable within two or three years.

Part 3

THE CRITICS

Introduction

The following selections are representative critical responses to Saroyan's short fiction. Saroyan, as the discussion in Part 1 indicates, was frequently criticized in reviews and articles by leftist and formalist critics in the 1930s and 1940s. Philip Rahv's review of *The Daring Young Man on the Flying Trapeze*, which appeared in *Partisan Review* shortly after the novel was published, is an example of Saroyan's treatment by the critical Left. Rahv's points are carefully argued, formulating a position that, on its own terms, would be difficult to answer.

In spite of Saroyan's popularity and his reputation among writers, he has seldom been welcome in the academy, which is probably the way he wanted it. One imagines that neo-Aristotelians and reader-response theorists would be as unable to deal with his work—sympathetically at least—as the New Critics were. Nonetheless, Saroyan's writings have generated a formidable amount of scholarly and critical work, some of it of a very high order.

Frederick I. Carpenter's "The Time of William Saroyan's Life" helps define Saroyan's relationship to the Emersonian and Whitmanic traditions in American culture. David Stephen Calonne discusses Anderson's role in Saroyan's career. Howard R. Floan deals with *My Name Is Aram* as "Saroyan's most serious bid for a single book that might prove representative of his achievement in short fiction." And Harry Keyishian compares Saroyan with Michael Arlen, the other well-known Armenian writer working in English during the first half of the twentieth century. Nona Balakian's "The World of William Saroyan" provides a solid introduction to various ethical and ethnic dimensions in Saroyan's work. In the passage reprinted here from "Whatever Happened to Saroyan?" William J. Fisher considers Saroyan's work within the political context of the 1930s. In "The Dark Side of Saroyan," the final critical piece reprinted here, Harry Keyishian addresses the side of Saroyan's work that many readers attracted to his whimsy and sentiment perhaps prefer to overlook.

Philip Rahv

Just because Saroyan has been writing silly letters to the magazines is no reason for discounting him as a total loss. First the common run of reviewers lost their heads and then the boys with the higher standards tried to laugh him out of court, and they almost succeeded. They pierced through the ballyhoo and pointed to his very definite shortcomings, his adolescent struttings, etc.; yet I feel that the man illustrates a literary trend or symptom of social importance. And this, rather than the efforts of press-agents or the rakish angle of his hat, explains the languishments whose blatancy so offended the adverse commentators. Except in a certain sense, both the response to him and what he says are not fads but articulations of concrete history. Hence it might prove worth while to examine his work in detail. Esthetics may be the undersea level of ideology, but that's where you find the pearls.

From the viewpoint of sheer writing Saroyan's performance deserves little praise. He overstates what he says and he says it the same way at the beginning, the middle and the end of his stories, self-consciously, with the romanticism of an uncalled-for defiance that soon becomes ridiculous. Usually he runs around and around a perception till finally it's as big as life and he can't miss it. Instead of philosophical overtones or implications, he gives us philosophy in the actual texture, line after line. He does not tread the earth; he promenades—a soul-de-luxe in felt slippers.

And yet there are many vivid passages in the book, which prove the writer to possess a very tangible talent. Moreover, since we don't believe "sheer writing" to be self-determining, it must be in the conception, in the world-feeling that shapes it, that we will find the source which mars his expression. In most of the stories Saroyan is concerned with himself, with his fusion with God and the Universe, with his dark ways as a young man of a dark kind. And these are precisely the stories that most perceptive critics didn't care for. He is more successful where

"Narcissus" (review of *The Daring Young Man on the Flying Trapeze*), *Partisan Review* 2 (June 1935): 84–85. Reprinted by permission of Betty T. Rahv.

he manages to discard the poetry of ego and eternity in favor of a more objective field of reference. Instances of this are *Laughter, Harry,* and *Aspirin Is A Member of the N.R.A.*, in which he tries to spread himself but the N.R.A.—more real than he—rudely overshadows him. The less there is of Saroyan as a subject (because then the subject ceases to exist and the writing really becomes "sheer writing") the less he writes "for God" and, ultimately, for *Vanity Fair.*

The dashing title of the book has given people a false sense of the author. Actually he is trembling. Objective life terrifies him—art alone is "everlastingly dependable." Working as a teletype operator he feels that he is being murdered, and only in the fiction room of the public library is he able to identify himself. He hates to think of the world's structure and events in it and change and strife; hence he denies its motion, seeking to affirm it as *being* in the Platonic sense, as a virtual stability "out of time": in other words out of history, which is social time. Then certainly it becomes necessary to lift Man (not men) "from the nightmare of history to the calm dream of his own soul." And this calm dream is "language" (not apprehension and expression as affective communication). For a while he is forced to give up writing because of poverty, and at once he "becomes nothing, not even a shadow." The real world presses in on him, and he cannot help feeling that "it is blasphemous for any living man" to live thus and that "he has less honor than a grocer's clerk, less dignity than the doorman at the St. Francis hotel, less identity than the driver of a taxi-cab." Here is the vision of shame in the face of the worker's labor, which proves its reality by affecting life. But it is merely a passing insight; its impingement on the consciousness is too brief to save him from the seductive mystery of the dream of *stasis.* It is easier, more in the tradition to rejoice in one's cosmic piety and fondle the typewriter thinking: "*This is my room and I have created a small civilization in this room, and this place is the universe to me. . . .*" Life from the Viewpoint of the Short Story! Now we can understand the sources of the prose, which is so prolix, naive and egocentric. Piece by piece a full portrait emerges. Without awareness he writes in one context: "Drama is impossible because everyone is interested in himself." This means that literature is impossible. A sensitive young man leaped into the eternal ether and was smothered.

I have seldom read a more self-revealing exposition of the life of the declassed intellectual, who, being an artist, finds in his very medium a haven from activity. The result is language without perception. He desires "evil," but all he finds is "filthiness"; he wants to give purity, but all he gives is the sentimentality of the "vastest ego." In the title-story he suffers starvation, he makes the rounds looking for work: but the resolution comes when he faints away into infinity. Rejecting on one side the brutishness and sycophancy of commerce, of getting ahead in the world, and on the other the sober courage of struggle against the prevailing oppression—what is left but consoling oneself with the small explosions of "universal" anarchism. He sees the existing order for what it is, for he comes "upon strange specimens of life, men made frightening by capitalism." Yet he cannot see how this same force makes "strange specimens" out of his own themes. In a letter to the *New Masses* he finds the Communist program the most valid, but that is, after all, a secular matter. As regards his writing, it is predetermined and immutable.

This whole mode, of course, is nothing new in American literature. But now the time is ripe for its stagnation; in Saroyan the whole stream comes to the surface; its peculiar essence has become marketable. In the historical sense the school of esthetes-modernists—from whom Saroyan stems and whose "holy" names he invokes in his little testaments—is philosophically of the same complexion. His masters had the advantage over him in functioning earlier, when the mode had a stronger base because of the absence, in the cultural sphere at least, of its dialectic opponent and conqueror. In the nineteen-twenties Horace Gregory quavered:

> And if you hear me crying: My god, my god, my god,
> down streets and alleys
> I am merely trembling (afraid, my god, my god,
> to be nothing to fade away,
> In grass, in stone.)
>
> *(McAlpin Garfinkel, Poet)*

But even then Gregory was half-aware, he turned it off and on, and has now moved away. Saroyan has made this the *leitmotif* of his first book, and the pseudo-intellectuals read him in wonder, for here at last is the mystery of Pound and Jolas and Cummings and Williams wriggling on the ground, in full view. Will he stay?

Frederick I. Carpenter

Of all American authors who have achieved fame since 1930, William Saroyan is perhaps the most original, the most versatile, and closest to the mood of the common people. His stories, his plays, and his novels have not only achieved popularity with the reading public, but have appealed vividly to that public which does not usually read. Some professional book reviewers also have acclaimed him. But at the same time, other professional reviewers have expressed a hearty disapproval. And, strikingly, every serious literary critic who has discussed his writing in book or in essay form has enthusiastically damned William Saroyan. The abyss in America between popular opinion on the one hand, and critical judgment on the other, has never been illustrated more graphically.

Of course there are good reasons for the critics' disapproval. Even Saroyan's best work is faulty, and very little of his work is "best." The bulk of his writing, although vivid, is careless and formless. His many volumes of stories contain few masterpieces, and much third-rate material. His plays are amorphous; and many of his prefaces are bumptious. He has produced, I think, only two really first-rate things: *The Human Comedy*, and a one-page preface to *The Time of Your Life*. Judged by purely literary and artistic standards, the formal critics are often right in condemning him.

But Saroyan's obvious artistic faults do not explain the hostility of the formal critics. All of them have specifically attacked his "morality" or his "philosophy." Grouping him with "The Boys in the Back Room," Edmund Wilson deprecated his "barroom philosophy." Philip Rahv used his writing to illustrate the "decay of values and taste,"[1] in modern literature. Edwin Berry Burgum—certainly no reactionary—described him as evidencing a "flight from maturity and responsibility."[2] And Joseph Remenyi characterized Saroyan as "a sentimental

"The Time of William Saroyan's Life," *Pacific Spectator* 1 (Winter 1947): 88–96. Reprinted by permission of American Council of Learned Societies. Copyright 1947 by the Pacific Coast Committee for the Humanities.

romanticist."³ If these critics grudgingly admitted the vitality of his work, they had little good to say of its intellectual or moral qualities.

Yet it is just these intellectual and moral qualities which make Saroyan's work most interesting and most important. If he were merely a romantic and sensationalist, we might dismiss him as a second- or third-rater. But the fact that he arouses such enthusiasm combined with such hostility suggests that he has something important to say.

In his artistic and moral faults and virtues alike, Saroyan suggests comparison with Walt Whitman. Like Whitman, he is an American "natural." Like Whitman, he celebrates himself and his America, but above all the America of his dreams. Not only his personality and his method suggest the good gray poet, but most of all his philosophy and his moral values are those of Whitman, Emerson, and the American transcendental tradition.

But obviously Saroyan is no traditionalist. Rather he is a product of the California of the twentieth century. If he seems to repeat the pattern of transcendental individualism, it is because that pattern has again become natural to the time and place in which he lives. Certainly he is as closely akin to the other California writers of his time—to Steinbeck, Sinclair, and Jeffers—as he is to Emerson and Whitman. For contemporary California has produced a school of writing which may well be called "the new transcendentalism." Seen in relation to the transcendental past and to the Californian present, William Saroyan takes on new stature.

I

If the most striking thing about Saroyan's writing is its originality, the most striking thing about Saroyan himself is his egotism. He shows a whole-hearted contempt for other people's rules, for society's customs, and for traditional values. In his prefaces he appears almost insolent. But this same egotism makes his creative writing fresh, vivid, and exciting. In the realm of morals, or philosophy, it creates an emphasis on the "transcendental" values of individual freedom and integrity. Perhaps Saroyan's combination of egotism, originality, and integrity may best be described by the old phrase: "self-reliance."

Saroyan's self-reliance produces much the same impression that Emerson's and Whitman's did a century ago. Indeed his first and most famous story repeated the theme of Emerson's early poem, "Goodbye, proud world! I'm going home." The daring young writer of the

1930's ventured forth to an employment agency, learned that the work-a-day world considered "writing" a mechanical and somewhat anomalous occupation, and returned home to live on the flying trapeze of the imagination. But his story made dramatic the contrast between the worldly values, and the esthetic or spiritual values of "writing." And this conflict of values has motivated all his subsequent work.

Indeed, another early story ironically entitled, *Love, Death, Sacrifice and So Forth*, developed this moral conflict in more general terms and commented on it explicitly. The traditional ethics of a Hollywood movie which the "writer" had witnessed not only seemed utterly conventional to him but contrasted with the reality which he had observed. Therefore, he generalized, "A long while back we made the rules, and now, after all these years,we wonder if they are the genuine ones, or if, maybe, we didn't make a mistake at the outset." Following this idea, Saroyan devoted most of his early writing to satirizing the conventional "rules," or values, of worldly society. If his later writing has been devoted more to the imagining and illustrating of new "rules" better fitted to a modern, democratic society, the negative struggle against all convention and all "society" came first.

Opposing himself to "the world," Saroyan exaggerated his ego, just as Emerson and Whitman did a century before him. "Vastest of all is the ego, the germ of humanity, from which is born God and the universe, heaven and hell . . ." he declaimed. And speaking personally, in preface after preface, he repeated, "I discovered that the rules were wrong. The trouble was, they had been leaving me out . . . so I made some new rules." And he repeated Emerson's old idea in different words: "The greater your faith [in yourself], the greater your talent." If Saroyan were not primarily a writer of fiction, able to clothe his transcendental ideas in the imaginative reality of human character and action, one might easily dismiss him as a mere disciple of Emerson and Whitman. But where Emerson had dealt with abstract ideas, and Whitman had applied them poetically and personally, Saroyan has written authentic fiction. Only in prefaces and in occasional short stories has he stopped at mere personal self-assertion.

And even in his earlier stories Saroyan often illustrated the positive values of integrity and self-knowledge, without which "self-reliance" remains mere egotism. *The Man With the French Post Cards*, for instance, described a down-and-out gambler who preserved his "integrity" at last by *not* selling pornographic pictures. A later story, *War and Peace*, told of a pitiful young misfit who finally won peace of mind by facing down his own problems and by understanding himself. All the characters of Saroyan's best play, *The Time of Your Life*, achieved happiness by doing what they wished most to do. So a stage direction described them: "The atmosphere is now one of warm, natural, American ease; every man . . . doing what he believes he should do, or what he must do. There is a deep American naïveté and faith in the behavior of each person." That Saroyan's characters are usually failures makes little difference; they realize the "inalienable" (but often alienated) American rights of "life, liberty, and the pursuit of happiness."

As he has developed, Saroyan seems to have become increasingly conscious of this peculiarly "American" quality of the "rules," or values, which his fiction has illustrated. After producing *My Heart's in the Highlands*, he observed with rare humility, "I am now five years an American writer. Several weeks an American playwright. Yet all I know is that I have not so much as made a real beginning." And he stated clearly the task ahead of him: "The imperative requirement of our time is to restore faith to the mass and integrity to the individual."

II

If Saroyan's early writings were mostly devoted to the assertion and fictional realization of the "integrity of the individual," his later writings have emphasized the value of "faith to the mass," or of belief in social democracy to all Americans. Not only have his values become more clearly defined, but they have become more social. The most successful realization of them occurs in *The Human Comedy*. The best statement of them appears in the prologue to *The Time of Your Life*. Since this prologue sums up his whole democratic philosophy, it may be read in full:

> In the time of your life, live—so that in that good time there shall be no ugliness or death for yourself or for any life your life touches. Seek goodness everywhere, and when it is found, bring it out of its hiding-place and let it be free and unashamed. Place in matter and in flesh the least of the values, for these are the things that hold death and must pass away. Discover in all things that which shines and is beyond corruption. Encourage virtue in whatever heart it may have been driven into secrecy and sorrow by the shame and terror of the world. Ignore the obvious, for it is unworthy of the clear eye and the kindly heart. Be the inferior of no man, nor of any man be the superior. Remember that every man is a variation of yourself.

No man's guilt is not yours, nor is any man's innocence a thing apart. Despise evil and ungodliness, but not men of ungodliness or evil. These, understand. Have no shame in being kindly and gentle, but if the time comes in the time of your life to kill, kill and have no regret. In the time of your life, live—so that in that wondrous time you shall not add to the misery and sorrow of the world, but shall smile to the infinite delight and mystery of it.

Where Saroyan's earlier writing was often rebellious and negative, his later writing has become almost wholly positive: "In the time of your life, *live*!" Indeed he may have tended to "accentuate the positive" too much. But he has also tended increasingly to face the problem of evil, and has made clear—both in his prefaces and in his fiction—that he belongs to the *interbellum* generation, when "the time comes to kill." Living in this time he has sought to reaffirm the old American faith, and even in war to treat all men as brothers and equals. In this also he recalls the faith of Walt Whitman during the Civil War.

But this transcendental optimism which Saroyan reaffirms is more than a faith; it is also an American philosophy of equality. All men are equal; under the skin "every man is a variation of yourself." Like Whitman, Saroyan has sought to convert this idea into reality through the chemistry of the creative imagination, not only embracing all men with a vague, cosmic sympathy, but imagining individual characters who realize the ideal values stated in the prologue. Thus the actors in *The Human Comedy* observe and suffer the misery of the world, but also live fully and smile at the infinite delight of it. In so doing they realize the old American democratic faith in new ways.

The Human Comedy is more than a miscellaneous collection of short stories about the Macauley family, or a whimsical exercise in autobiography. It is a carefully constructed book, describing the growth to emotional maturity of a typical American boy, through four clearly-defined stages. If the chapters resemble short stories in construction, they are all focused on a single purpose. And if intrusions of the old irresponsible whimsy appear (as in the "Speech on the Human Nose") they follow a definite design. Moreover, interwoven suggestions of myth and symbolism tend to raise the particular and personal to the realm of the universal.

Perhaps the most interesting and original character of this *Comedy* is not the boy, Homer, but the manager of the telegraph office, Spangler, whose ultimate function seems to be "to restore faith to the mass." A breezy, utterly American young man, who dislikes to wear neckties, both his name and his actions nevertheless constitute him a living refutation of Spangler's philosophy of pessimism, and an interpreter of what Emerson called "the beneficent illusions of the universe." Yet this Spangler never loses his personal identity as the official employer and human companion of young Homer.

If Homer Macauley of Ithaca, California, is a typical young American boy, he is also heir to all the world's civilization. As the book opens he has just left home to work for the local telegraph office. Because his father is dead, and his older brother is in the army, he feels a vague emptiness. But in Spangler he finds a substitute father and older brother, all in one. And from his mother he learns faith in life: "It doesn't make any difference, because I *believe*."

But when Homer later returns to school, he confronts social evil and injustice. His track coach is a snob who treats him unfairly, and tries to give his protégé, Hubert Ackley III, special privileges. Opposing this injustice, Homer's history teacher explains to him the American principle of equality: "Every man in the world *is* better than someone else, and not as good as someone *else*. . . . In a democratic state every man is the equal of every other man up to the point of exertion, and after that every man is free to exert himself to do good or not. . . ." Inspired by her advice, Homer is vaguely moved to try to change the world: "The ideas I get," he said. "A different world, a better world, a better people, a better way of doing things." And then he realizes: "Yeah, I guess I've changed all right. I guess I've grown up."

But this is only the half of it. In the second part of *The Human Comedy*, Homer Macauley confronts natural evil, and learns that there are evils inherent in human nature which personal effort and social progress cannot change. "Death, Don't Go to Ithaca" introduces a series of illustrations of natural and human perversity: boys stealing green apricots and a child unreasonably demanding "cookies—raisins in"; grown-ups indulging in travel as an escape from life, women selling themselves for money, and men making themselves "half-human, half-dead," like the fantastic Mr. Mechano. All this causes Homer to exclaim, "I thought a fellow would never cry when he got to be grown up, but it seems that's when a fellow starts, because that's when a fellow starts finding out about things." But a letter from his brother, Marcus, warns him that he must face the facts of death and evil by learning to "live, in the years of your life, forever."

Because Homer Macauley has learned to fight against social evil, but to meet the inevitable fact of natural evil in the only way it can be met—by living as fully as possible; and because he has learned faith from his mother and brother and from Spangler, he is finally ready to accept the news of his brother's death as an adult, and to comfort his mother and older sister, rather than the reverse. And he is able consciously to adopt his brother's friend, Tobey, into the family, just as he had unconsciously adopted Spangler as a substitute for his dead father.

Thus *The Human Comedy* describes how a typical American boy goes out from his home, experiences the injustices of the world and fights against them, experiences the evils of human nature and learns to accept them, and finally achieves a mature faith not founded on childish optimism. Unlike the adolescent "young man on the flying trapeze," he does not retreat from the world to indulge in romantic self-pity; nor, on the other hand, does he abandon his self-reliant independence or his faith in human nature. Rather, he carries his self-reliance over into the world of society, and tempers his faith by the facts of experience. Saroyan's hero achieves maturity, not through rebellious self-reliance, nor through any desperate conformity to convention, but through a gradual realization of the old American faith in one's self and one's fellow men.

III

But William Saroyan remains the least bookish and the least traditional of contemporary American writers. His material is drawn from living experience with his California environment and from the living traditions of his immigrant family. His style, for better or for worse, is utterly colloquial, instinctive and unliterary; if he has ever read Emerson, he gives no hint of it, and he sounds his democratic yawp without benefit of Whitman. He remains an American natural, whose similarities to writers living or dead are entirely coincidental. Here is no question of literary influence. And yet the similarities remain.

The time and the place of William Saroyan's life (let us repeat) is twentieth-century California. His fiction is peopled with vineyard workers, suburban householders, wandering laborers, barflies, insurance salesmen, newsboys, evangelists, and back-porch philosophers—with all the colorful kaleidoscope of human beings who make up a California community. These live with the optimistic insecurity of a people on the make, a people struggling and starving, falling and bouncing up again and never despairing. In this California a failure is only an opportunity for a fresh start, and all things are always possible. ". . . [T]he world," says Mrs. Macauley, "waits to be made over by each man who inhabits it, and is made over every morning like a bed."

William Saroyan's actual California, that is, resembles very closely Emerson's actual New England and Whitman's actual Manhattan of a century ago. Therefore, it has inspired the same feelings in its people and the same ideas in its writers. "Nature is not fixed, but fluid" in Los Angeles and Fresno today, just as it was in Boston and Concord a century ago. For both societies are young, recently past their pioneering days, and both are imbued with the progressive spirit of adolescence, groping toward the articulation of new and exciting ideas. Both believe that "all things are possible," because in a new, unsettled society almost all things really are possible. Therefore the literatures of both exhibit a bold self-reliance combined with a bumptious self-assertion. At best, both suggest the feeling that there *is* something new under the sun. At worst, they produce the painfully self-conscious posturing of a Saroyan or a Whitman boasting of his own greatness.

At worst, both Saroyan and Whitman belong to "the lunatic fringe" of this "transcendental" ferment. For modern California has produced the same medley of "Muggletonians, come-outers . . . men with beards and philosophers," that Emerson once observed in New England. Upton Sinclair and his "Utopians," seeking to reform the world, are related to Saroyan's heroes. The Oriental mysticism of Gerald Heard and Aldous Huxley, and the "saturnalia of faith" proclaimed by the California revivalists have further confirmed the religious faith which Saroyan inherited from his Armenian family. And the air of "unreality" (observed by so many people in southern California) which made credible the feats of *The Flying Yorkshireman* (who needed only faith in order to soar at will through space) has also made credible the feats of *The Daring Young Man on the Flying Trapeze*. But with this distinction: Saroyan's "flying trapeze" is firmly anchored to the rafters of this unfinished California society, whereas the utopians, the theosophists, and the fantasists belong to that homeless, floating population which is half Hollywood and half imported European intelligentsia.

At best Saroyan's fiction gives expression to a philosophy of life which is typically Californian, and also is central to the American transcendental tradition. Unlike the muckraking and socialistic writing of Upton Sinclair, Saroyan has no axe to grind, no gospel to preach. Unlike the naturalistic and sociological fiction of John Steinbeck, Saroyan treats human nature and social injustice without violence and anger. But because he rejects the utopian socialism of Sinclair and the revolutionary violence of Steinbeck, Saroyan does not adopt the pessimistic nihilism of Robinson Jeffers. Rather he reaffirms the old American faith of Emerson and Whitman, who, skeptical both of social reformers and of prophets of doom, proclaimed that the world could be reformed only by reforming the individual, and that this could not be accomplished by social compulsion and physical violence but only by personal freedom and loving tolerance. "Build therefore your own world."

William Saroyan has not yet realized the full potentialities of his talent. His work has often been shoddy and his idealism fuzzy. But he has shown a capacity for steady growth, both in art and in thought. He is firmly rooted in the rich soil of his California reality. And he has absorbed—no matter by what mysterious processes of photosynthesis—the ideal truths of the American tradition. Far from being a decadent sensationalist or immature romantic, he has progressively realized a consistent American philosophy and has steadily advanced toward individual maturity and toward social responsibility.

Notes

1. Philip Rahv, "William Saroyan: A Minority Report," *American Mercury* 57 (September 1943), 371–77.

2. Edwin Berry Burgum, "The Lonesome Young Man on the Flying Trapeze," *Virginia Quarterly Review* 20 (Summer 1944), 392–403.

3. Joseph Remenyi, "William Saroyan: A Portrait," *College English* 6 (November 1944), 92–100.

David Stephen Calonne

The need to deny tradition and influence is common among writers, particularly at the beginning of their careers. Yet Saroyan's first book was profoundly affected by the work of other writers, Sherwood Anderson's in particular. Malcolm Cowley has written that Anderson was a "writer's writer, the only story teller of his generation who left his mark on the style and vision of the generation that followed. Hemingway, Faulkner, Wolfe, Steinbeck, Caldwell, Saroyan, Henry Miller . . . each of these owes an unmistakable debt to Anderson, and their names might stand for dozens of others."[1] Indeed, the "style and vision" of Anderson's *Winesburg, Ohio* are readily discernible in many of the stories of *The Daring Young Man on the Flying Trapeze*.

Anderson's famous story-cycle supplied Saroyan with a precedent for exploring the search for identity as well as a style which exhibited the very virtues of "ease and freedom" which he so highly valued. In the story "Sophistication," Anderson had described the painful struggle of George Willard into manhood in simple, clear sentences.

> George Willard, the Ohio Village boy, was fast growing into manhood and new thoughts had been coming into his mind. All that day, amid the jam of people at the Fair, he had gone about feeling lonely. He was about to leave Winesburg to go away to some city where he hoped to get work on a city newspaper and he felt grown up. The mood that had taken possession of him was a thing known to men and unknown to boys. He felt old and a little tired. Memories awoke in him. To his mind his new sense of maturity set him apart, made of him a half-tragic figure. He wanted someone to understand the feeling that had taken possession of him after his mother's death.
>
> There is a time in the life of every boy when he for the first time takes the backward view of life. Perhaps that is the moment when he crosses the line into manhood.[2]

Excerpted from *William Saroyan: My Real Work Is Being* by David Stephen Calonne (Chapel Hill: University of North Carolina Press, 1983), 18–21. © 1983 by the University of North Carolina Press. Reprinted by permission.

128

The powerful influence of Anderson on Saroyan's literary sensibility can be seen in the story "And Man."

> With the beginning of spring that year came the faint and frag-
> mentary beginning of this thought, burning in my mind with the
> sound of fire eating substance, sweeping through my blood with the
> impatience and impetuosity of a deluge. Before the beginning of
> this thought I had been nothing more than a small and sullen boy,
> moving through the moments of my life with anger and fear and
> bitterness and doubt, wanting desperately to know the meaning and
> never quite being able to do so. But now in November I was as large
> physically as a man, larger, for that matter, than most men. It was
> as if I had leaped suddenly from the form of myself as a boy to the
> vaster form of myself as a man, and to the vaster meaning of myself
> as something specific and alive.[3]

It is clear from a comparison of these two passages that Saroyan had been deeply affected by Anderson's prose rhythms and themes. Although the "ease" of expression in both passages is obvious, Saroyan tends to move away from Anderson's bare, reportorial syntax toward a more lyrical and intense phrasing: "the sound of fire eating substance, sweeping through my blood with the impatience and impetuosity of a deluge." Thematically, both stories take place in late fall, and both concentrate on a moment of awareness in the lives of boys who self-consciously look back at their own process of growth.

This intense focusing on a single instant of illumination when a character suddenly perceives the hidden reaches of reality, becomes aware of things as they are, links Saroyan most profoundly to Anderson's work. In the passage above, this perception occurs as an opposition—boy/man—which is typical of Saroyan's dichotomous vision of experience. But more important, as Roger Asselineau has remarked, both stories contain "a poetic epiphany in the course of which we are suddenly brought into contact with the inexpressible mystery of life."[4]

We find another such epiphanic moment of experience during which time seems frozen in "The Earth, Day, Night, Self." Here Saroyan presents a young man contemplating his pregnant girlfriend and the child that is slowly growing within her: "He saw the earth growing in her through him, the universe falling into the boundaries of the form of man, the face, the eyes, solidity, motion, articulation, then awareness, then quiet talk, quiet communion, himself again, and yet another, to proceed through time, one day, one night, the earth, and the energy of man, himself. . . . He began to laugh softly, touching the girl where it was growing, feeling fine" (p. 177). These fissures in time during which characters experience true being through relation to Other and to the cosmos, when the despair or fullness of their lives is revealed to them, occur throughout *The Daring Young Man on the Flying Trapeze.*

In Saroyan's book, as in *Winesburg, Ohio,* many of the characters feel despair more often than wholeness. Like the "grotesques" of Anderson's small town, they are, as James D. Hart has remarked, "puzzled, groping, baffled, and possess no vision of order or channel for directing their energies against the frustrations of contemporary existence."[5] In Saroyan's Fresno, California, we meet many people like those who live in Winesburg. For example, in the story "Seventeen," the young man Sam Wolinsky "wanted to do something. A feeling of violence was in him, and he was thinking of himself as something enormous in the world. He felt drunk with strength that had accumulated from the first moment of his life to the moment he was now living, and he felt almost insane because of the strength" (p. 141). Sam is an adolescent trapped and overwhelmed by the powers of sexuality which are assailing him. He searches for a means by which to express his innermost self and meets only defeat and frustration. Like many adolescents and adults depicted in Saroyan's work, Sam is seeking not only the satisfaction of his lust but also a deep transformative experience through communion with another human being. He is seeking love, and also something ineffable, which is perhaps not available in human existence.

Notes

1. Anderson, *Winesburg, Ohio,* intro. by Malcolm Cowley, (New York: The Viking Press, 1958), 1.

2. Ibid., 233–34.

3. William Saroyan, *The Daring Young Man on the Flying Trapeze* (New York: Random House, 1934), 92.

4. Asselineau, *The Transcendental Constant in American Literature* (New York: New York University Press, 1980), 134.

5. Hart, *The Oxford Companion to American Literature* (Oxford University Press), 33.

Howard R. Floan

My Name is Aram (1940) . . . is Saroyan's most serious bid for a single book that might prove representative of his achievement in short fiction. By this time he had evolved a style of swiftness and simplicity, an ability to select images both strikingly concrete and richly suggestive, and to create sharply visualized scenes without retarding the forward movement of his stories. It had been an arduous process of learning to know his most fruitful subject and to trust those techniques most natural to him. It may be surprising to speak of a new confidence in one whose brashness as a young writer was unrivaled, but the introduction to *Aram* contains a note of confidence that is quite different from the braggadocio and posturing of his earlier prefaces. He acknowledges his debts freely, not only to Edward Weeks and Edward J. O'Brien for their encouragement, but to Fresno for providing him with "an abundance of material by nature so rich in the elements of comedy as to require little or no labor to select and chronicle." Nothing in the book is entirely fiction, he says; no member of his family is fully there, but no one is fully absent. The ease and sincerity of these tributes imply the strength of his realization that, although the people of *Aram* sprang from his remembered past, they bore the uniqueness of *his* imagination and temperament and possessed their life and meaning only because he had worked out an adequate technique for turning the facts of personal history into the truths of fiction. "All humanity" is in the "proud and angry Saroyans," he says, and one can see "the large comic world" in the little city of Fresno.[1]

In writing of children Saroyan placed himself in an old and prominent tradition of American literature. There are ideological moorings for *Aram* in Ralph Waldo Emerson, who expressed a philosophical respect for childhood by assuring authors that a little girl or a "couple of school-boys" could bring them closer to truth than could the epic sub-

Excerpted from *William Saroyan* by Howard R. Floan (Boston: Twayne, 1966), 81–84. © 1966 by Twayne Publishers, Inc. Reprinted by permission of Twayne Publishers, a division of G. K. Hall & Co., Boston.

jects of the world. The American Transcendentalists agreed with William Wordsworth that the child is closer to nature and therefore to God than is man. Though later in the nineteenth century the bad boy became popular in fiction, it was a temporary countermovement within the family rather than a new strain. The bad boy was not really bad; he was just an irritant to a society that had become overly concerned with respectability. There has never been an American line of descent from Lazarillo de Tormes or Moll Flanders or other young people of European literature whose aim was to learn the rules of an adult world, no matter how corrupt, so that they could adapt to its ways and prosper. Instead, American writers have emphasized the shock and recoil of the young in their first awareness of evil. From Nathaniel Hawthorne, Henry James, Stephen Crane, and Mark Twain, to Ernest Hemingway, Carson McCullers, and J. D. Salinger, American writers have postulated a division between youth and age and have generally assumed the essential goodness of children and their superiority and incorruptibility because of this innocence. Huck Finn escaped corruption and finally withdrew beyond the domesticating reach of society. The pain of initiation left Nick Adams scarred, Holden Caulfield emotionally disturbed, and Frankie Addams permanently aware of her essential aloneness. But who would doubt their continued decency?

What sets Saroyan apart from the mainline of this tradition, contrary to popular assumptions, is not the innocence of his children or their apparent immunity to evil. The difference relates to the conflicts in his stories, which do not derive from adult-child polarities but from contradictory impulses within the heart of man. Saroyan was aware of Mark Twain's great achievement in presenting society through the eyes of a boy, for *Huckleberry Finn* was one of his favorite books; and some of Saroyan's earlier stories, such as "The War" and "The Oranges," turn on the child's resentment of the indifference, inadequacy, and cruelty of adults. In turning away from this obviously fertile field, however, he was instinctively following a tack more suitable to his qualities of mind and more intimately a part of his own experience. *Little Children*, as I have pointed out, presents the immigrant and his children in the difficult process of becoming Americanized; but its social criticism, though valid and significant, is only a by-product of the author's unerring sense of the way things were. This was life in the valley, he is saying; I am sharing it honestly; see what it means.

With *My Name is Aram* Saroyan became more conscious of an age-old, universal aspect of the subject before his eyes: the conflicting claims of dream and reality had a very personal meaning for people who had severed ties with home and country to come half-way around the world in search of a new life. They had found that the "Golden West" was not an eldorado or a paradise but simply a place to live, good enough if they worked hard. Moreover, enough time had passed for them to achieve some tranquility and resignation in weighing the validity of hope against the constant pull of disappointment. In such an environment the poetic and the practical seemed to have genealogies of their own and were visible in distinct personalities. It required time and the perspective of distance for Saroyan to understand this spirit of his people and to know that it would provide him with more than a point of view: it would become his truest subject. To read his books in sequence from *The Daring Young Man on the Flying Trapeze* to *My Name is Aram* is to see how gradually but inevitably Saroyan found his way into this subject.

Thus *My Name is Aram* is not essentially about childhood. It seeks out instances of poetic involvement and develops them in relationship to the claims of the practical. Recognizing no essential difference between youth and age, it presents many adults who are forever childlike and some children who are never young. The narrator is an adult recalling his youth, and Aram is therefore both man and boy. To the extent that the pronoun of the book's title has a precise meaning, it refers to a residue of romantic responsiveness from the narrator's youth. In this sense the child is father to the man, a Wordsworthian dictum which, if it can be used outside the context of platonic idealism, means an awareness of continuity that strengthens the narrator's impression of self, not as subject but as reflector. (For the book is less about Aram than about other Garoghlanians, especially uncles, who make up the most memorable portraits.) Saroyan's feeling for life quickened as he turned back to the time and place of his boyhood.

Since Aram's actions and thoughts are recollected, the book sacrifices much of the suspense and vividness possible to contemporaneous reporting. It should not be judged finally in terms of conflict, though most of its stories have a dramatic structure and all of them place a poetic sensitivity in some kind of opposition to the demands of practicality. But Aram is never really involved in conflict; he learns nothing about himself or about his associates through a course of action: the recognition belongs to the mature mind in retrospect and inheres in its mood of nostalgia. The value of the book lies in the quality of its lyricism, where it should finally be judged. Though its lyricism cannot produce the vitality and sustaining force of dramatic tension, it does illuminate the more accessible pleasures of daily living. The book gives this kind of pleasure. And to its great credit, the mood of nostalgia, though indispensable to the speaker, does not transfer itself to the reader. Instead, the book evokes a feeling for the preciousness of the moment and a recognition of a continuing capacity for responsiveness such as one could never have known as a child. Thus the book escapes sentimentality, not through its comic strain, as is widely believed, but through the casual and unobtrusive way in which its major theme gives body and form to the individual stories and to the book as a whole. Though not profound or complex, it is an intellectually respectable theme, and in *Aram* Saroyan has made it appear inseparable from its subject and from the technique of retrospect.

Note

1. *My Name Is Aram* (New York, 1940), vii–x.

Harry Keyishian

For all the striking differences, [Michael] Arlen and [William] Saroyan did . . . share the experience of being Armenian. For both, it was a powerful factor in shaping their attitudes, in terms of the positive elements of Armenian culture and family life and the adjustments their being Armenian forced on them. For both, the latter were, at times, noticeably bitter.

In *The London Venture* Arlen described some of the difficulties of going to an English public school while bearing a lengthy Armenian name, and remarked that even as an adult he was made to feel, by acquaintances, that being Armenian was "something of a *faux pas*." In an entertaining and revealing short story, "Confessions of a Naturalized Englishman," which appeared in the collection *Babes in the Wood* (1929), Arlen's narrator—a young man who has been "stood up" by a girl who had promised to meet him for dinner—associates his failures in love, life, and career with being Armenian: "What nonsense they were—my strivings, my hopes, my ambitions! . . . What art could come from an Armenian? What greatness—what, even, of worth? O Armenia . . . The peoples of the West are unable any longer to wring any pleasure from pitying you. They are bored with your Christianity, with your massacres, with your complaints, with your existence." The fortunes of the narrator do rise by the end of the story, but hardly due to a triumph of national pride! Rather, Arlen has revealed the bitterness and self-hatred he apparently felt as a young man of (temporarily) thwarted ambitions, when he was made to feel like an alien in a land from which he sought and needed acceptance.

D. H. Lawrence portrayed that bitterness in the character Michaelis, based on Arlen, in *Lady Chatterley's Lover* (1929). Lawrence and Arlen had met in Florence in 1927—met again, more accurately, since they

Excerpted from "Michael Arlen and William Saroyan: Armenian Ethnicity and the Writer," in *The Old Century and the New: Essays in Honor of Charles Angoff,* ed. Alfred Rosa (Rutherford, N.J.: Fairleigh Dickinson University Press, 1979), 202–6. © 1978 by Associated University Presses, Inc. Reprinted by permission of Associated University Presses.

had been acquainted in 1915–16—while Arlen was suffering a decline in reputation after the fading of *The Green Hat* from the best-seller lists. Lawrence was then writing the third version of *Lady Chatterley*. After his meetings with Arlen, Michaelis was created, an Irish playwright who had achieved great success, but who had been turned on viciously by the public when his vogue had passed. Michaelis "pined to be where he didn't belong. . . among the English upper classes. And how they enjoyed the various kicks they got at him! And how he hated them!" Assuming that Lawrence's insights are valid (and not just a projection of his own feelings), one concludes that Arlen hated from a comfortable distance: he lived on the French Riviera through the 1930s.

But the label of "foreigner" stuck with Arlen, even during World War II. In 1940 he patriotically accepted the post of public relations officer for the Western Midlands Region. He endured the bombing of Coventry and wrote feelingly of the devastation and of the gallant efforts of the townspeople to carry on in the wake of disaster. But very shortly Arlen became the subject of a "question" in Parliament: an imbecile MP from Birmingham found it objectionable that a "Bulgarian"—as Arlen indeed was, by birth—should hold such a position of trust in wartime. He resigned his post early in 1941 and left England shortly after.

Arlen moved to the United States. His funds had been sequestered in England for the duration of the war, so he went to Hollywood where he did some screenwriting and saw his short story, "Gay Falcon," get turned into a series of pleasant and profitable mystery movies (the "Falcon" series, for RKO) starring George Sanders and Tom Conway. He settled in New York after the war, where his life appeared to be a pleasant round of lunches with friends and celebrities at various comfortable New York restaurants. We have the eloquent testimony of his son, Michael J. Arlen, in his book *Exiles* (1969), that those years were also troubled and frustrating; but to his public—what was left of it, at least—Arlen behaved with a grace befitting his successful and stylish life. One hopes that he felt, at last, at home. He died in New York in 1956.

Like Arlen, Saroyan—in the vastly different terrain of Fresno—had to deal as a child with hostility directed at him due to his national background. In *The Bicycle Rider in Beverly Hills* he comments: "If you were an Armenian in Fresno, this was an enormous fact about you, of special importance, and you had no choice but to carry the fact of it in one of two ways: proudly or even arrogantly, or shyly (if not secretly), and with embarrassment." The Armenians of Fresno, he continues, "were considered not only foreigners, but unattractive foreigners." Hence, he either had to be prepared to be belittled—which he wasn't—or else to "meet contempt with contempt." And so unlike Arlen, who outwardly at least courted acceptance most of his life, Saroyan says he "despised those Armenian boys who toadied to 'the American.'" Only later in the century was it possible for Armenians to be neither arrogant nor embarrassed, but "to be indifferent instead, but that needed time." For Arlen, as shown above, that time never really came.

Both men, then, had to contend with the feeling of being "foreign." Each responded in a way that seemed proper for his personality and his situation. Each paid a price, in terms of personal discomfort; but each reaped the benefit of heightened insight and intensified compassion. In Arlen's work one sees the effects in his vivid depiction of outsiders—of rebels, underdogs, and criminals. In Saroyan the effect is more obvious and more diffuse: it appears in his memorable depictions of Armenian-American life and in his own restless and continuing search for identity.

In one respect Saroyan has a vast advantage. Being born in the United States, he never had to face the legal problems of being an alien; and he also has a more concrete sense of physical landscape and his relation to it. But, more importantly, his experiences were broadly recognized as a common feature of American life. As Oscar Handlin points out in *The Uprooted*, his study of the history and meaning of immigration in the United States, America "was the land of separated men. . . . The newcomers were on the way toward being Americans almost before they stepped off the boat, because their own experience of displacement had already introduced them to what was essential in the situation of Americans." Saroyan's Armenian background, in other words, made him all the more authentically American, and his sense of alienation was, ultimately, a bond rather than a barrier.

Both Arlen and Saroyan lived their creative lives with courage, accepting the terms their societies imposed and putting their considerable literary talents on the line in their struggle for recognition. They did not, in the process, establish literary models for Anglo-Armenians or Armenian-Americans to follow, but they display in broader and more useful terms the human capacity to cope with and prosper in hostile surroundings, and to do so with style.

137

Nona Balakian

What can one say about William Saroyan that he himself cannot say better? Does one need to analyze a rainbow? Should one try to explicate Cézanne? Does it really enhance our enjoyment of a work of Mozart or Chopin to explain how they achieve their effects? Saroyan has a way of defeating his critics even before they begin. And this is why, after an astonishingly prolific career spanning more than forty years, Saroyan has remained virtually untouched by literary historians or critics and why to this day there is no standard edition of his works.

That fact in itself is my challenge in venturing to explore the Saroyan phenomenon and, by bringing together the various threads of his achievement, to reveal him to readers in a new way.

Like so many others, undoubtedly, I have been reading Saroyan or seeing his plays in bits and pieces over the years. (I recall that I wrote an article titled "Saroyan Prescribes 'The Time of Your Life'" in my college magazine.) To this day you will find his work in all kinds of publications: in the *Ladies' Home Journal*, the *New York Times* (Op-Ed or Sunday Book Review), *Harper's*, the *Atlantic*, the *New Yorker* and even *TV Guide*. Recently the Shirtsleeve Theatre produced a new play of his, *The Rebirth Celebration of the Human Race at Artie Zabala's Off Broadway Theatre*, and in the fall of 1975 John Houseman's Acting Company brought us that longtime classic, his 1939 Pulitzer Prize play, *The Time of Your Life*. Not to forget the Armenian Diocese's production in the winter of 1975 of a new play, *The Armenians*, which some of us were fortunate to catch in its short run. An autobiographical work, *Sons Come and Go but Mothers Hang in Forever*, was published in the summer of 1976.

We listen to Saroyan, we watch, we read—now with a sense of enchantment, now with disappointment (no writer can be so prolific and remain always in top form), but most often with refreshment—as he restores harmony and wholeness to our sight—and then we go on to

Excerpted from "The World of William Saroyan," in *Critical Encounters: Literary Views and Reviews, 1953–1977* by Nona Balakian (Indianapolis: Bobbs-Merrill, 1978), 162–70. © 1978 by Nona Balakian. Reprinted by permission of Macmillan Publishing Co.

something else: usually these days to something more involved, full of confusion and dissonance and unresolvable, sticky modern problems. In this intermittent awareness of Saroyan, we tend to glimpse and remember certain repeated motifs, in themselves not always so significant: we invariably seize on the *ethnic* subject—the wacky uncles and cousins, the sly old-country humor, the desperate need to be moral about life. Or, depending on our taste and inclination, we will wallow in—or be put off by—his unabashed belief in the goodness of man, by his childlike delight in being alive and disconnected with the larger world and its turmoil. Still others—the critics, for instance—will wonder that there is still so much vitality left in the old boy, when his younger contemporaries, J. D. Salinger, Jack Kerouac, Carson McCullers and Truman Capote, either are dead or have virtually given up writing.

It is only when one reads Saroyan continuously over a period of time that one can come to a true estimate of his stature as a writer, apart from the particular things one loves in him. Only then can one begin to find an explanation for his inexhaustible creativity and for the secret of his durability in this somber era of the twentieth century.

Saroyan has written reams about his own work in his prefaces to his stories and plays, most of it more distracting than useful to a critic. But nothing he has written is as revealing as the statement he makes in the preface to his ballet-play, "The Great American Goof," from his 1941 book *Razzle-Dazzle*.

"Nobody other than myself," he wrote, "seems to understand that the world is not real. That in reality there is no such thing as the world. There is, of course, but I mean for all practical purposes; when I say practical I mean poetic and wonderful. The world which everyone other than myself seems to have identified and accepted as the World is in reality a figment in a nightmare of an idiot. No one could possibly create anything more surrealistic and unbelievable than the world which everyone believes is real and is trying hard to inhabit. *The job of art, I say, is to make a world which can be inhabited.*"

He goes on to say in this preface that while he ignores the world deliberately, he keeps a clear eye on it all the time. "The style in our day," he continues, "is to save the world in every poem we write. . . . But probably the most any man can ever save or has a right to save is himself." "What I say is, what world? Where do you see any world?"

You cannot be in Saroyan's presence for any length of time without realizing that in his own life, his own person, he has remained true to the beliefs and ideals that informed his work from the beginning. There was never a character more Saroyanesque than Saroyan himself today. If anything, he is more emphatically himself than he ever was. With this difference: As a young man there was brashness and bravado in the way he let his faith be known. The world had still to humble him—he was aware that it would, for the world spared no one, least of all the sensitive. Uttered in his late sixties, the brash remark (if there is one) is followed by a knowing chuckle, as if he were not denying what he said but winking at the way he was saying it, only to emphasize his point: that life has meaning, that art and literature are the best means we have of expressing that meaning, that a dignified survival for any of us, but especially for the artist, matters more than anything else.

Let me digress here for a moment to tell a little about the Saroyan I saw in the summer of 1975 in his Paris surroundings. I was traveling with my sister, the writer Anna Balakian, and her daughter Suzanne, in both of whom Saroyan found kindred spirits. Never solemn, least of all when he is mouthing solemn truths, Saroyan at once put us at ease: a great talker, he is also a good listener, and because he seems to sense what in particular will interest those in his company, there is continual give and take. In his simply, casually furnished walk-up apartment near the Opéra, where he spends several months of the year (those times he is away from Fresno, California), the books and papers are neatly piled, ready to be referred to. Drinking tea with him there, or later over Schweppes (he hardly ever touches alcohol these days), or casually talking over instant coffee in the Paris office of the *New York Times*— on all these occasions, he appeared the soul of affability, spreading the contagion of his warmth, of his unfailing good humor.

Not that the reflective, the serious side was missing: talking about his new plays (and he has a stack of them which he will not show to publishers or producers), he deplores the present state of the American theater, which he blames essentially on the commercialization of the arts in general, and also on agents, editors and reviewers. There are hints of outrage, of anger held in check—for he remains a man who cares. But underneath it all is a benign acceptance of life's vicissitudes if not of their power to crush the individual. Unencumbered by material possessions, still keeping alive memories of the Fresno-Armenian oasis of his early youth, while at the same time never losing hold on the present moment, with whatever demands it makes on him, he is a new kind of mystic, a free spirit who knows life's true worth and has retained his zest for doing what he can to cause it to be revealed.

140

In Saroyan's denial of the world there is none of the elitist escapism of the expatriates of the twenties. Saroyan is not involved in any experimental literary group; he simply does his work, looks around, communicates *silently* with the natives (for though he understands French, he makes little effort to speak it). He waves to the little boy leaning out of a window across the street and waits to see him wave back—a sign of their common humanity. If anything, on this alien soil, his American quality is more than ever pronounced. It is reflected not only in his dress, which is casual and comfortable (even baggy), in his Western American accent and extravagance of expression, but in more subtle ways that speak of his need always to be himself, to put the most ordinary stranger at ease, to deflate pomposity, and to expect nothing less than the impossible. Indeed, one is tempted to conclude that the source of Saroyan's optimism is his assimilation of the American stance—the *original* American, of course, with his inborn faith in "life, liberty and the pursuit of happiness."

But if that alone were its source, why would he stand out as a maverick? The unaffiliated beatniks and flower children of the fifties, racing their way on the road, their backs turned on an oppressive Establishment, seemed also to be created in the original American mold. What essential lack of faith led them down the road to disillusionment, with specious escape in drugs, in asocial acts? If Saroyan's optimism is more firmly embedded, one suspects it is because it derives not from escape from the self but from head-on confrontation with it. Those wacky and unreconstructed Armenian uncles and cousins, those misfits and losers on whom Saroyan centers his affection, are never romanticized "noble savages," as some critics have suggested. Think of the idealistic father, the unpublished poet in *My Heart's in the Highlands*, or Homer's mother in *The Human Comedy*, and all those innumerable Saroyan children: innocents they may be and quite unsophisticated in the ways of the world, but they have manners and insights that suggest they relate to their fellow men: they are too innately cultured to be mistaken for "savages."

In one of his earliest stories in *The Daring Young Man on the Flying Trapeze*, Saroyan says: "I cannot resist the temptation to mock any law which is designed to hamper the spirit of man."

The word to watch for in that sentence is "spirit." He wants the spirit of man, what renders him human, to be protected from the corrupting pressures of society. And the proof of this lies in the fact that these special rebels of Saroyan—call them "spiritual rebels"—do not deny the home, repudiate the family or community: they do not shun their neighbors or denounce the pleasures of simple fellowship. Quite the contrary, Saroyan's people seem to exist for the purpose of establishing the fraternity of man.

And then there is, of course, Saroyan's ethnic dimension. Paradoxical though it may seem, no influence on Saroyan has done more to reinforce his claim as an American writer than his Armenian heritage and background.[1] (I speak here again of an earlier American style, not the contemporary, which has absorbed so many foreign influences.) Saroyan's childhood experiences among his uninhibited, colorful Fresno-Armenians have left a significant impact not only on his character but on the very manner of his storytelling. I refer to that often long-winded, indirect manner of the Eastern *massal* or long tale (e.g., "The Thousand and One Arabian Nights"), always at its best when it reflects the idiosyncrasy of the teller's personality. If in Saroyan this does not stand out as a foreignism, it is because it blends so well with another tradition, the American Western oral tradition (used so effectively before him by writers like Mark Twain and Ring Lardner), which Saroyan absorbed through his reading and environment. In addition, as a child in the circle of his extended family, he fell under the spell of the fable, which in turn drew him to allegory and that extra dimension of reality which as a young idealist he set out to discover. Here again, an influence in his *American* environment turns the fable's impact into a moral force. Though he often refers to himself as a mystic (and speaks of the *mystery* of religion), the specific religious references in his work are of the Presbyterian church where he attended Sunday School and briefly sang in the choir. To this day, he sings these hymns with affectionate reverence.

There were other moral forces in his early years that combined the American and Armenian influences. There was the example of his immigrant widowed mother, struggling to keep the family alive; there was the historic proof of man's tenacity to survive in the heroic story of his own Armenian people. The Armenians' suffering and endurance through the centuries inevitably fused in his mind with the agony of a world on the brink of world war and the deep gloom of America's demeaning Depression years. The years when he was emerging as a writer—the middle thirties—were a time of leveling off: white-collar workers, laborers, professionals mingled in a common pursuit for subsistence. Economic pressures drew people closer together as they sought solace in friendship, relief in humor, and hope in love. Having been brought up to cherish these things, Saroyan sought from his earliest stories to bring a more mystical apprehension to the American Dream. He wrote in 1934: "I am a propagandist, and in this very story I am trying to restore man to his natural dignity and gentleness. I want to restore man to himself. I want to send him from the mob to his own body and mind. I want to lift him from the nightmare of history to the calm dream of his own soul, the true chronicle of his kind."

Rereading *The Daring Young Man on the Flying Trapeze*, one is struck by the essential solemnity underlying the work as a whole: the cosmic consciousness and the rhetoric it unleashes contain echoes of Sherwood Anderson and Thomas Wolfe, with an occasional departure into the tight-lipped Hemingway. The characteristic Saroyan humor has not yet emerged from under the weight of romantic naturalism. But with successive volumes of his stories—*Inhale, Exhale, Three Times Three, Little Children*, and *My Name Is Aram*—Saroyan learned to detach himself from his characters, or, rather, to keep a certain distance from them, in order to empathize with a broader spectrum of humanity.

Reviewers of these early books were generally charmed by the variety and appeal of his ethnic characters, by the refreshing absence of political and sociological preaching in a time when "the movement" was on everyone's lips, by the warm-hearted humor and the hope for humanity his stories generated. Later, the more literal-minded of the critics grew impatient, even bored, since instead of inventing new plots and dramatic situations Saroyan reworked his material, improvising variations on certain basic themes.

Parenthetically, let me say here that Saroyan (who loves music of every sort) loves particularly to listen to Chopin; this he does in Paris on an ancient victrola that leaves much of the music to one's imagination. Interesting—because I have thought of his stories in terms of music like Chopin's, which moves from a fixed center toward limits that are foreordained yet curiously liberating in their essential sameness. In the preface to a short play, "Opera, Opera," he wrote: "The truth of art is the truth of emotion, not intellect. Emotion and intellect are essentially or eventually inseparable, and the quality of one depends on the quality of the other." Behind that emotion is a fixed vision of the human potential—an ideal—which most of us, in the process of living, often lose sight of. To keep that vision alive, he repeatedly places before our eyes fragments of what he calls "a world which can be inhabited."

"What was the human race I discovered in Fresno?" he asks in "The Home of the Human Race." "It was my family, my neighbors, my friends, the teachers at the school, the classmates, the strangers in the streets, and myself, most of all myself." And he goes on: "Were the strangers any good at all? Was it possible to believe them at all? They *were* good: good and hopeless, and that is why I discovered art, for I did not want them to be hopeless." Only through art, he knew, could their dignity be preserved.

Saroyan's innocents are not only children—though children are among his best creations. Among the adult innocents are the noncon-formists, nonmilitant eccentrics, like the uncle who decided to grow pomegranates in the desert, undaunted by warnings of inevitable fail-ure; they are also the unconditioned young people who let their hearts dictate their actions, like the young girl in a prison kitchen who re-sponds to a prisoner's anguished call in his play *Hello, Out There!* They are the "losers" who hang on, like the writer Rock Wagram in his 1951 novel of that name, living by the "lies of his art that wink and tell him he is the one." But best of all, though sometimes barely believable, are the deliberate innocents—the free spirits who turn their backs on the materialistic world to cultivate compassion, beauty, love, whole-ness, humor.

Even more than courage, it is humor that sustains these free spirits. Humor in Saroyan's human family is a saving grace, the balm that heals, the lifeline that leaves fear and disenchantment behind. Again and again, the realist and the mystic go hand in hand to create a sense of absurdity in the differences that separate the mundane world from his own way of seeing it. Through his ever-present sense of man's mor-tality, Saroyan keeps his eye fixed on the natural world, that rich, true, earthy place on the other side of the artificial Human Comedy, where there are no roles to be enacted and a person's true style is allowed to emerge.

Note

1. In a recent review in the *New York Times Book Review*, Edward Hoag-land takes note of the fact that Saroyan "has been a profoundly innovative 'ethnic' writer—one of the very first in America." What needs to be added in this connection is that Saroyan was the very first ethnic writer to carry the ethnic element into the universal. It is in the naturalness and ease with which he achieves this transmutation that Saroyan's originality lies.

William J. Fisher

When Saroyan's stories began appearing in the early 1930's, the literature of the day was somber with gloom or protest. And though Saroyan's fiction was also born of the Depression, often telling of desperate men, of writers dying in poverty, it nevertheless managed a dreamy affirmation. Politically and economically blind, Saroyan declared himself bent on a one-man crusade in behalf of the "lost imagination in America." In an era of group-consciousness, he was "trying to restore man to his natural dignity and gentleness." "I want to restore man to himself," he said. "I want to send him from the mob to his own body and mind. I want to lift him from the nightmare of history to the calm dream of his own soul."

This concept of restored individuality governed Saroyan's principal attitudes, his impulsive iconoclasm as well as his lyrical optimism. While Saroyan joined the protestants in damning the traditional villains—war, money, the success cult, standardization—he was really attacking the depersonalization which such forces had effected. He was just as much opposed to regimentation in protest literature as in everyday life. ("Everybody in America is organized except E. E. Cummings," he complained.) Writing about foreigners and exiles, the meek and isolated, "the despised and rejected," he celebrated the "kingdom within" each man. The artists in his stories preserved a crucial part of themselves; there was spiritual survival and triumph, let economics fall where it might. And in the glowing stories about men close to the earth of their vineyards, about glad children and fertile, generous women, Saroyan was affirming what he called the "poetry of life" and exalted with capital-letter stress: Love, Humor, Art, Imagination, Hope, Integrity.

In effect, Saroyan was restoring the perspective without which the writers of the thirties had often (for obvious reasons) reduced the in-

Excerpted from "Whatever Happened to Saroyan?" *College English* 16 (March 1955): 337. © 1955 by the National Council of Teachers of English. Reprinted by permission of the National Council of Teachers of English.

dividual potential to a materialism of physical survival. When a character in one of his plays insisted that food, lodging, and clothes were the only realities, another responded, "What you say is true. The things you've named are all precious—if you haven't got them. But if you have, or if you can get them, they aren't." However limiting Saroyan's simplifications might prove, they none the less contained important truths which had been lost sight of amidst the earnestness of agitation-propaganda. If Saroyan is given any place in future literary histories, he should be credited with helping to relax ideologically calcified attitudes.

Harry Keyishian

In "Not Waving but Drowning" by the English poet Stevie Smith, a man drowns while a crowd watches. The problem was that the swimmer had a reputation for enjoying himself: "he always loved larking." And so nobody paid attention to his frantic efforts to signal for help. After he was dead, people finally understood that he hadn't been cheerfully waving, but sending a quite different message: "I was much further out than you thought / And not waving but drowning." Indeed, that had been true for a long while before: "I was too far out all my life / And not waving but drowning." Like the swimmer in the poem, William Saroyan also seemed all his life to "love larking," and so we were eager to see him as he presented himself: brash, confident, optimistic. The adjective "Saroyanesque" was coined to describe his particular freewheeling style of expression.

And yet if we had really looked, if we had been reading him attentively, especially in his later years, we had to see that the other side of him, the dark and troubled side that existed in constant tension with his "upbeat" pose. The latter always won out, rhetorically: he insisted on the victory of creativity and optimism. But that does not absolve us, as his readers, from understanding that it is not in the conclusions he reached but in the struggle he endured that we will find truths he has to tell. The essence of Saroyan lies in that dialectic, the oscillation between hope and despair, wishes and fears, joy and tragedy.

Of course there had been a pessimistic streak in his work from the start. After all, the protagonist of his first celebrated short story, "The Daring Young Man," *does* die. But it was not until the early 50's that this darker side began to dominate. In the collection *The Assyrian and Other Stories* (1950) and the novels *Rock Wagram* (1951) and *The Laughing Matter* Saroyan confronted human failure, loss and limitation. At the same time, his work became a search for compensations for mortality. He sought restoration in memories of his youth, his relationship with

"The Dark Side of Saroyan," *Ararat: A Quarterly* 25 (Spring 1984): 47–49. © 1984 by the Armenian General Benevolent Union. Reprinted by permission of Harry Keyishian.

his children, certain healing actions—like bicycle riding—and, above all, writing itself.

In 1963 *Not Dying* described the period of depression, during which the author is haunted by premonitions of his own death. Saroyan tries to adopt a proper stance, "to accept the messages with grace." He is rescued from these feelings when his son and daughter visit him in Paris. They play cards, quarrel, make up, talk about writing, go to the movies; they discuss the proper way to behave and to be. His son complains about him:

> You drink and gamble and keep bad hours and all that stuff, and you aren't a very good friend, you don't really have any friends at all, according to what I've heard. You speak in the loudest voice I've ever heard. You dominate every group I've ever seen you in. You almost never seem interested in anybody else, unless it's an attractive woman. You're very swift and rude with people you don't like. You're self-centered, arrogant, vain, vulgar, and really very ignorant—you know less about the details of what's going on in the world, for instance, than even I do, and you don't care anything about that, either, you don't think that that is any reason why you can't explain everything to everybody, including experts. You make people nervous and uncomfortable just by being among them. You're always clearing your throat and spitting if you're in the street, or burying the stuff in a handkerchief if you're indoors. And a lot more. So how can you believe you are a good man?

Since it is unlikely that Aram, his real son, could have produced such a cogent and detailed analysis at the age he is supposed to be here, it is clear that Saroyan is really projecting, trying to imagine what he must seem like to his son. So these are really "charges" that Saroyan makes against himself. How does he answer them?

Earlier in the book, Saroyan had described what writing had meant to him, how it had changed him, as a person, for the better: "I used to believe my face was coarse, for instance, but after I had finished writing something, I noticed that my face was suddenly no longer coarse. The work had changed me so powerfully inside that you could see it in my face, which was still the same face, but no longer coarse." And here, in answer to his son's fictional accusations, he gives a similar answer: "I . . . believe that my writing, whenever it turns out to be good, is good because it is written by a good man."

These conversations, and, more important, the writing of the book itself, save him from his feelings of depression and mortality: "I began to write the book so that the writing of it could take the place of dying, of my own literal death." Saved by involvement with family and craft, he gets moving again. "I went to work and wrote a play for money. I didn't die."

Saroyan's swings of mood are evident in these passages. On the one hand, there is self-consciousness, self-doubt, awareness of his shortcomings; on the other hand, there is pride in what he is and what he does and the way he goes about his business of being Saroyan. First, forebodings of doom and mortality; then, the exhilaration of accomplishment.

In a later book, *Sons Come and Go, Mothers Hang in Forever* (1976), Saroyan again expressed the anguished intensity he projected as a young celebrity, an intensity that frightened people off: "I had long known that there was something about me that was either violent or frightening for some reason. In certain three-sided clothing store images I had for some years come upon myself, with shock and disbelief, regret and shame, disappointment and despair, for I am indeed clearly violent, mad, and ugly, all because of intensity of some kind, a tension, an obsession with getting everything that there was to be got, a passion, an insanity." He wonders how to "cast out the demon" that was in him, "or at the very least how to . . . keep it quiet and not so terribly noticeable."

But at the same time, Saroyan sees his "incivility" as a saving force: "I have always been a Laugher," he wrote in *Sons Come and Go*, "disturbing people who are not laughers, upsetting whole audiences at theatres. . . . I laugh, that's all. I love to laugh. Laughter to me is being alive. I have had rotten times, and I have laughed through them. Even in the midst of the very worst times I have laughed."

Tragically, the discrepancy Saroyan felt between what he hoped to be and what he feared he was crept into his relations with his children. We know too well the solemn accusation Aram makes in *Last Rites*— "He wanted me to die"—but we must wonder at the accuracy of that perception when we read, in *Sons Come and Go*, of Saroyan's pained awareness of his inability to make his true feelings known to those closest to him, to his children. Saroyan describes his despair as he listens to a tape recording he made of a conversation with Aram and Lucy when they were seven and four: "I was abashed by the monster I had clearly been—loud, swift, impatient, unable to slow down, unable to be disciplined enough to make serene my nearness to each child, alone with me in an office. I sounded insensitive to them, and yet, this is the terrible and puzzling thing, I had been full of nothing but profound love, easy intelligence, abundant comedy, enormous health—and yet unmistakeably a monster." Perhaps this passage makes it easier for us to credit Aram's account of his father's apparent hostility towards him; but we must also see the anguish of the father, torn between the wish to love, simply, directly, and spontaneously, and his inability to express that love.

Keeping that failure of communication in mind, we can well understand Saroyan's deep admiration for George Jean Nathan, the noted drama critic who was Saroyan's booster, friend, and teacher. In *Sons Come and Go* Saroyan remarks that Nathan: "never had anything *instructive* to say about the *writing* of plays, but knew more about the theatre than anybody else I have ever talked with. He passed along what he knew in a way that was easy for me to take or leave. And his talk both invited and compelled participation on my part, and the part of anybody else who happened to be at the table." So what Saroyan could not do for his son, Nathan had been able to do for him; and that created, in Saroyan, a sense of gratitude and awe.

There was also his admiration for Nathan's style, for in that too Saroyan saw exemplified qualities he wished he had: "He dressed neatly and he went out among the thieves and assassins. . . . And everything he wrote had a laughter in it. He was one of the most serious men in the living world . . . but he refused to burden his writing, or his readers, with the agony of his unconverted and apparently indestructible soul." Saroyan concludes, "There can't ever be anybody like him again."

Was Nathan really such a paragon, or is this only Saroyan's hero-worship? We cannot say. What does emerge from these lines, however, is a sense of what Saroyan held precious, and seemed to see in his admired friend: the ability to combine in one personality the capacity for laughter and seriousness; the ability to have and convey knowledge; the style that permitted a person to walk untouched among "thieves and assassins."

The conflict between the energies of life and the undeniable fact of mortality is the focus of *Obituaries* (1979), the book in which he used the 1976 necrology list in *Variety* for an extended commentary, memoir, and meditation. Although he was never a man of traditional pieties or orthodox religious beliefs, it nevertheless startles us to read his head-on confrontation with the finality of death—all death, his own included:

> A stiff is found in bed, bereft of sleep and dream, and God knows where the person has gone, some say to heaven, some say to hell, some say only to graveyard, some say back to nature. . . . I don't believe in such silly stuff as going to heaven to sit on the right hand of somebody fictitious and damned foolish, or going to hell to be roasted by someone else even more fantastic and silly—just dump my beloved ashes . . . into the raging ocean, which as you know, as you surely remember, was the character of my soul, and the style of my eight minutes of dances, songs, and witty sayings.

But we will be startled only if we have failed to hear what Saroyan has been telling us right along. "Don't tell me I'm sentimental, you sons of bitches," he roared elsewhere in *Obituaries*. Indeed, there was sentiment in him. But sentiment was only one part of his personality, and he wills and compels us to understand his wholeness—his spiritual and his physical hungers, his idealistic and his pragmatic sides; he demands that we understand his lifelong dissatisfaction with himself, the people he knew, the life he lived, and the terms of existence itself.

If we would honor Saroyan, we must strive to understand him, to confront what he strove to tell us. We must not codify him, but treat his writing for what it was, a dynamic product of the interplay between the opposing forces within him. In this is revealed not only the meaning, but the courage of his confrontation with life.

Chronology

1890s   Members of the Saroyan family begin emigrating from Bitlis, in what is now eastern Turkey, to the United States.

1905   Armenak Saroyan arrives in the United States.

1908   William Saroyan born in Fresno, California, on 31 August, the fourth and last child of Armenak and Takoohi Saroyan. Named for Dr. William Stonehill, who had aided Armenian refugees.

1911   Armenak dies. Saroyan, his brother, and his two sisters are sent to the Fred Finch Orphanage in Oakland, California.

1916   The Saroyan children return to their mother in Fresno, where they spend the rest of their childhood.

1925   Saroyan leaves high school without graduating.

1926   Moves to San Francisco.

1928   Story accepted by *Overland Monthly*. At an uncle's suggestion, he tries living in New York but does not like the city and returns to San Francisco.

1932   Begins long association contributing to the *Hairenik* publications in Boston.

1934   "The Daring Young Man on the Flying Trapeze" and "Seventy Thousand Assyrians" published in *Story* magazine. *The Daring Young Man on the Flying Trapeze and Other Stories* published in October.

1935   Visits Soviet Armenia for the first time.

1936   Works for the B. P. Schulberg studio in Hollywood. *Inhale and Exhale* and *Three Times Three* published.

1937   *Little Children* published.

1938   *Love, Here Is My Hat* and *The Trouble with Tigers* published.

1939   *Peace, It's Wonderful* published. *My Heart's in the Highlands* produced in New York. Writes *The Time of Your Life*.

1940   *The Time of Your Life* produced on Broadway and awarded a Pulitzer Prize, which Saroyan rejects. *My Name Is Aram* published.

1941 *Saroyan's Fables* published.

1942 Drafted into army.

1943 *The Human Comedy* published. Marries Carol Marcus. Son, Aram, born.

1944 *Dear Baby* published.

1945 Leaves army.

1946 *The Adventures of Wesley Jackson* published. Daughter, Lucy, born.

1949 Divorced. Gambling losses. Problems with Internal Revenue Service.

1950 *The Assyrian and Other Stories* published. Takoohi Saroyan dies. *The Twin Adventures* published.

1951 Saroyan remarries Carol Marcus.

1952 Second divorce.

1956 *The Whole Voyald and Other Stories* published.

1961 Buys apartment in Paris at 74, rue Taitbout.

1971 *Letters from 74 rue Taitbout* published.

1981 Dies 18 May in Fresno. Half his ashes are buried in Fresno, the other half in the Armenian Pantheon in Yerevan, Soviet Armenia.

1988 *Madness in the Family,* edited by Leo Hamalian, published.

Selected Bibliography

Primary Works

Short Story Collections   This list includes only first American editions, not paperback reprints, English editions, or translations. Those other kinds of editions are listed in David Kherdian, *A Bibliography of William Saroyan: 1934–1964* (San Francisco: Roger Beacham, 1965).

The Assyrian and Other Stories. New York: Harcourt, Brace, 1950. Includes "The Assyrian," "The Parsley Garden," "The Theological Student," "The Plot," "The Foreigner," "The Poet at Home," "The Third Day after Christmas," "The Pheasant Hunter," "The Cornet Players," "The Cocktail Party," and "The Leaf Thief."

The Daring Young Man on the Flying Trapeze and Other Stories. New York: Random House, 1934. Includes "The Daring Young Man on the Flying Trapeze," "Seventy Thousand Assyrians," "Among the Lost," "Myself upon the Earth," "Love, Death, Sacrifice, and So Forth," "1, 2, 3, 4, 5, 6, 7, 8," "And Man," "A Curved Line," "Snake," "Big Valley Vineyard," "Aspirin Is a Member of the N.R.A.," "Seventeen," "A Cold Day," "The Earth, Day, Night, Self," "Harry," "Laughter," "The Big Tree Coming," "Dear Greta Garbo," "The Man with the French Post Cards," "Three Stories," "Love," "War," "Sleep in Unheavenly Peace," "Fight Your Own War," "Common Prayer," and "The Shepherd's Daughter."

Dear Baby. New York: Harcourt, Brace, 1944. Includes "Dear Baby," "The Hummingbird That Lived through Winter," "The Stolen Bicycle," "Knife-like, Flower-like, Like Nothing at All in the World," "The Dream," "A Time of Genius," "The Story of the Young Man and the Mouse," "The Struggle of Jim Patros with Death," "Sailing down the Chesapeake," "I Know You Good," "My Witness Witnesseth," "The Flashlight," "How It Is to Be," "Mr. Fleming and the Seven Wonders of the World," "Passengers to Europe," "The Declaration of War," "Highway America," "My Home, My Home," "The Grapes," and "The Faraway Night."

The Human Comedy. New York: Harcourt, Brace, 1943. *Note*: Although *The Human Comedy* was published as a novel, this study argues that its model is *Winesburg, Ohio*, and that consequently it is in some ways a collection of short stories.

Selected Bibliography

Inhale and Exhale. New York: Random House, 1936. Includes "Resurrection of a Life," "Five Ripe Pears," "The World & the Theater," "Laura, Immortal," "The Oranges," "Morning," "The Younger Brother," "London, Ah, London," "The Living Multitude," "The Gay & Melancholy Flux," "Two Days Wasted in Kansas City," "The Bridge," "Going Home," "A Night of Nothing," "The Drinkers," "The Horses & the Sea," "World Wilderness of Time Lost," "The Broken Wheel," "The War," "The Death of Children," "Daily News," "Our Friends the Mice," "The Symphony," "Raisins," "The Barber Whose Uncle Had His Head Bitten off by a Circus Tiger," "Yea & Amen," "Solo for Tin Gazoo," "Prelude to an American Symphony," "How Pleasant to Have Passed through Buffalo," "The Drunkard," "My Picture in the Paper," "Nine Million Years Ago," "Memoirs of a Veteran Actor," "A Tipped Hat to the Lamp Post," "With a Hey Nonny Nonny," "I Can't Put Two & Two Together," "Secrets in Alexandria," "Hunger Laughing," "The Mother," "Panorama Unmerciful," "The Great Unwritten American Novel," "Antranik of Armenia," "Six Hundred and Sixty-six," "The International Song of the Machine Gun," "Taxi to Laughter & Life Unending," "Poem, Story, Novel," "The Revolution," "Little Miss Universe," "Solemn Advice to a Young Man about to Accept Undertaking as a Profession," "Two Thousand Four Hundred and Some Odd Dollars for Kindness," "An Occurrence at Izzy's," "Our Little Brown Brothers the Filipinos," "The Japanese Are Coming," "Ah-ha," "At Sundown," "Christians Singing," "Rain," "A Christmas Carol," "Psalms," "A Note on Travel," "The Dark Sea," "Malenka Manon," "The Proletarian at the Trap Drum," "The Black Tartars," "The Egg," "The Little Dog Laughed to See Such Sport," "Train Going," "The Whistle," "Finlandia," and "The Armenian & the Armenian."

Letters from 74 rue Taitbout, or Don't Go, but if You Must, Say Hello to Everybody. New York: World, 1969. Short stories or memoirs, depending on one's point of view.

Little Children. New York: Harcourt, Brace, 1937. Includes "Laughing Sam," "The Sunday Zepplin," "Corduroy Pants," "The Coldest Winter Since 1854," "O Higher Accountancy, O Traffic Management," "The Only Guy in Town," "The First Day of School," "The Man Who Got Fat," "Around the World with General Grant," "The Messenger," "Many Miles Per Hour," "The World's Champion Elevator Operator," " My Uncle and the Mexicans," "Countryman, How Do You Like America?," "The Crusader," "The Cat," and "Where I Come from People Are Polite."

Love, Here Is My Hat. New York: Modern Age Books, 1938. Includes "Love, Here Is My Hat," "Ever Fall in Love with a Midget?," "The Trains," "One of the Least Famous of the Great Love Affairs of History," "The La Salle Hotel in Chicago," "Gus the Gambler," "Saturday Night," "Coffee and Sandwiches at Louie's on Pacific Street," "Ah Life, Ah Death, Ah Music, Ah France, Ah Everything," "Three, Four, Shut the Door," "For My Part I'll Smoke a Good Ten Cent Cigar," "The Genius," "A Lady Named Caroline," "The Fire," "You're Breaking My Heart," "The Filipino and the Drunkard," "Jim Pemberton and His Boy Trigger," "War and Peace," "The Poor Heart," and "A Family of Three."

Madness in the Family. New York: New Directions, 1988. Includes "Madness in the Family," "Fire," "What a World, Said the Bicycle Rider," "Gaston," "The Inscribed Copy of the Kreutzer Sonata," "Picnic Time," "A Fresno Fable," "Lord Lugger of Cheer," "Cowards," "Najari Levon's Old Country Advice to the Young Americans on How to Live with a Snake," "Mystic Games," "Twenty Is the Greatest Time in Any Man's Life," "How the Barber Finally Got Himself into a Fable," "There Was a Young Lady of Perth," "How to Choose a Wife," "The Last Word Was Love," and "The Duel."

My Kind of Crazy Wonderful People: Seventeen Stories and a Play. New York: Harcourt, Brace & World, 1966. Previously published stories rewritten and simplified.

My Name Is Aram. New York: Harcourt, Brace, 1940. Includes "The Summer of the Beautiful White Horse," "The Journey to Hanford," "The Pomegranate Trees," "One of Our Future Poets, You Might Say," "The Fifty Yard Dash," "A Nice Old-fashioned Romance, with Love Lyrics and Everything," "My Cousin Dikran, the Orator," "The Presbyterian Choir Singers," "The Circus," "The Three Swimmers and the Grocer from Yale," "Locomotive 38, the Ojibway," "Old Country Advice to the American Traveler," and "The Poor and Burning Arab."

A Native American. San Francisco: G. Fields, 1938. Contents the same as in *My Name Is Aram.*

Peace, It's Wonderful. New York: Starling Press, 1939. Includes "The Greatest Country in the World," "The Insurance Salesman, the Peasant," "The Rug Merchant and the Potted Plant," "The Year of Heaven," "The Europa Club," "1924 Cadillac for Sale," "The Love-Kick," "Little Moral Tales from the Old Country," "The Warm, Quiet Valley of Home," "A Number of the Poor," "The Monumental Arena," "Peace, It's Wonderful," "Piano," "The Mouse," "The Adventures of a Young Man Some Day to Be Another Jack London," "Romance," "At the Chop Suey Joint on Larkin Street at Two Thirty in the Morning," "Ohio," "The War in Spain," "Comedy Is Where You Die and They Don't Bury You because You Can Still Walk," "Noonday Dark Enfolding Texas," "Johnny the Dreamer, Mary the Model at Magnin's, and Plato the Democrat," "The Best and Worst People and Things of 1938," "What We Want Is Love and Money," "The Sweet Singer of Omsk," "The Same as Twenty Years Ago," "The Russian Writer," and "The Journey and the Dream."

Selected Bibliography

Saroyan's Fables. New York: Harcourt, Brace, 1941. Includes "The Parable of the Loveliness of Faith in God and How It Saved the Life of One Good Man," "What the Intelligent Young Man Said of the Bird-brained Young King Who Thought It Was Funny to Assign People to Whimsical but Impossible Tasks," "How the Bear Took Pity on the Foolish Hunter Who Sold the Bear's Skin while It Still Surrounded the Bear," "The Meaningless but Beautifully Angry Remark of the Bear to His Friend on the Subject of Hypocrisy," "How the Pompous Remark of the Turtle Spoiled the Last Moments of the Lion Who Was Shot by a Hunter but Was Still Proud and Lonely," "How the Slightly Kind-hearted Husband Almost Lost His Wife," "What Happens if You Try to Satisfy Some People," " The Embarrassment That Came to the Crook from Odessa Who Tried to Swindle the Bright Boy of Bitlis," "The Tribulations of the Simple Husband Who Wanted Nothing More than to Eat Goose," "How the City Slicker Made a Monkey out of the King Who Thought He Was Too Smart to be Fooled by Anybody," "What the Armenian Butcher Said to the Armenian Barber without Speaking," "How the Devil Was Humiliated Three Times by the Young Native of Bitlis Who Never So Much as Went to School," "The Lies the Bald-headed Man and the Man with the Running Nose Told the Man with the Crooked Leg," "How the King Who Wanted to Believe the Blind of His Realm Were Nice People Got Back His Gold Coin," "The Surprise the Rabbit Got Who Imitated the Roaring Lion," "How the Mohammedan Period of Fasting Was Brought to an Official End because Now and Then Even a Handful of Deaf People Are Thrown Together by Humanity for the Purpose of Sending a Little Laughter down the Ages," "How the Dishonest Traders Outwitted Each Other but Died in the End Nevertheless," "What Happened to the Wise Guys Who Scoffed at the Family Man Whose Faith Was So Great That Even in Tragedy He Said, Praise God, He Knows What He Is Doing," "One of the Long and Confidential Prayers the Religious Old Armenian of Fresno Used to Make Every Wednesday Night at the First Armenian Church," "The Seven Instructive Words That Were Said to the Poor Man Who Was under the Impression that Being Poor Entitled Him Also to Be Slovenly," "What the Man Who Was Sometimes Crazy but Always a Democrat Said to the Young King Who Was Sometimes Bored but Always Willing to Listen," "How Difficult It Is for a Man to Enjoy Living if His Wife Is Socially Ambitious and Goes around Telling Fantastic Lies about His Clairvoyant Powers," "What the Priest Said to the Assassin Who Had Broken the Standard Rules for Inhuman Behavior," "How the Hair of Women Is Long, the Understanding Short, and What a Ghastly Lack of Appreciation There Is in Them for Genius," "The Problem of the Unhappy Little Boy Whose Father Regarded Him as a Child, Instead of a

Personality," "My Grandmother Lucy's Magnificent Parable of the Three Instructions," and "The Lovely Thing That Happened to the Beautiful Step-Daughter Who Was Cemented into the Tower by the Bad Step-Mother."

Three Times Three. Los Angeles: Conference Press, 1936. Includes "The Man with the Heart in the Highlands," "The Question," "The Living and the Dead," "Summertime," "Public Speech," "Life and Letters," "Baby," "The Beggars," and "Quarter, Half, Three-Quarter, and Whole Notes."

The Trouble with Tigers. New York: Harcourt, Brace, 1938. Includes "The Tiger," "Sweetheart Sweetheart Sweetheart," "The Brothers and the Sisters," "Another Summer," "The Way to Be Alive," "I Could Say Bella Bella," "The Nurse, the Angel, and the Daughter of the Gambler," "O.K., Baby, This Is the World," "It's Not as if We Don't Appreciate Your Kindness," "The Brokenhearted Comedian and the Girl Who Took the Place of His Unfaithful Wife," "On Malibu Bay," "A Scenario for Karl Marx," "The Legend Makers," "The Ants," "The Great Leapfrog Contest," "A Talk with Father," "The Acrobats," "Citizens of the Third Grade," "The People, Yes, and Then Again No," "Everything," "Woof Woof," "A Prayer for the Living," "Little Old New York," "The World," "A Letter to the Old City Editor," "A Clear Warm Day," "Memories of Paris," "The Job," "Some Day I'll Be a Millionaire Myself," "The Vision," "The Dale Carnegie Friend," "Anything for a Laugh," "A Nice Boy, Even if He Is Rich," "The Pool Game," and "We Want a Touchdown."

The Whole Voyald and Other Stories. Boston: Little, Brown, 1956. Includes "A Writer's Declaration," "The Home of the Human Race," "The Failure of Friends," "Love of London," "The Proud Poet," "The Idea in the Back of My Brother's Head," "The Winter Vineyard Workers," "The Rescue of the Perishing," "The Inventor and the Actress," "The Play That Got Away," "The Reader of *The World Almanac for 1944*," "A Visitor in the Piano Warehouse," "Palo," "The Rearward Dog," "The Return to the Pomegranate Trees," "Sit Down, Won't You," "Aram Saeetyujkfogl," "The Sea and the Small Boy," "Bill McGee's Brother," "Paris and Philadelphia," "The Armenian Writers," and "The Whole Voyald and Heaven Itself."

Selected Stories

Except as indicated these volumes merely reprint stories from earlier collections.

Best Stories of William Saroyan. London: Faber & Faber, 1942.

Selected Bibliography

The Man with the Heart in the Highlands. New York: Dell, 1968.

The Man with the Heart in the Highlands and Other Early Stories. New York: New Directions, 1989.

My Name is Saroyan. Edited by James H. Tashjian. New York: Harcourt Brace Jovanovich, 1983. This volume reprints all but a few miscellaneous pieces first published in *Hairenik Daily*, *Hairenik Weekly*, and *Armenian Review*. Many of the stories are reprinted for the first time in this volume. Some might better be classified as essays, though given Saroyan's very general definition of the story, they are listed as such here. They include "A Fist Fight for Armenia," "The Barber's Apprentice," "The Moment of Life," "Noneh," "Summer Laughter," "Explosion," "Home," "The Two Thieves," "The Poet," "Seven Fragments," "The Russian Singer," "The Young Husband and Father," "The Hours of Day and the Hours of Night," "The Body," "The Comic Page and Vital Statistics," "What You Get for Trying Your Best, if Anything," "The First Day of Summer," "Of Love and Time," "A Flash of the Flashlight and the World-shaking Question: 'Joe?,'" "The Ride on the Great Highway in the Sky of the Sinking Sun," "Seven Easy Ways to Make a Million Dollars," "Genesis," "Problems of Writing," "The Empty House," "Notes," "California," "A Moment of Prose in Kansas," "A Holy Silence," "The Unpublished Writer, Rain, and His Daughter," "The Word," "1933," "The Song," "Life, the Magazine, and Harry, the Polo Man Who Didn't Make the Team," "The Fable of the War between the Old Complex and the New Culture," "The Long Way to Tipperary," "The Life," "Cuba Libre," "The Last Summer," "The Watermelon Eater," "Axis," "When the Cow Came . . . ," "Two Long Novels, Condensed," "Lauri," "The Boy from Kingsburg," "The Small Trouble That Starts at Home," "The Man Who Was Born under the Sign of Scorpio," "A Couple of Miscellaneous Prophecies, More or Less Guaranteed to Come True," "Another Day, Another Dream," "Liberty, 5¢," "I'm Right, the World's Wrong," "My Financial Embarrassment," "The Wonderful World of Geniuses," "How They Got Rid of the Unwelcome and Greedy Visitor," "The Parachute Jump," "A Survivor of the Influenza Epidemic of 1918," "The Friends of the Monkeys," "Notes of Days Gone By," "My Grandmother Lucy Tells a Story without a Beginning, a Middle, or an End," "The Man Who Knew My Father as a Boy in Bitlis," "One Hello and One Goodbye," "A Moment of Freedom and Fun," "Hayastan and Charentz," "The Gambled Coat," and "My Shoes: a Short Story from 1933."

The New Saroyan Reader: A Connoisseur's Anthology of the Writings of William Saroyan. Edited by Brian Darwent. San Francisco: Donald S. Ellis, 1984.

The Saroyan Special: Selected Short Stories. New York: Harcourt, Brace, 1948.

The William Saroyan Reader. New York: G. Braziller, 1958.

Uncollected Stories

"The Actress and the Cop." *Saturday Evening Post,* 4 May 1959, 22–23.
"Ah-ha, the Cat Saw the Mouse." *Saturday Evening Post,* 27 February 1965, 70–72.
"Alive." *Ladies' Home Journal,* August 1964, 65–66.
"Around the World, and Death, and Back Again." *Reporter,* 4 June 1964, 31–34.
"The Armenian Mouse." *Ararat* 5 (Summer 1962): 2–6.
"Art; or, On Account of Orozco." *Américas* 7 (January 1955): 13–16.
"The Best Angel God Ever Saw." *Saturday Evening Post,* 16 November 1963, 94–95.
"A Big Plate of Rice and Meat Is Not Too Much for Me at All." *Boston University Journal* 23 (Winter 1975): 37–39.
"The Biggest Watermelon Anyone Ever Saw." *Saturday Evening Post,* 11 September 1965, 56–59.
"Bike." *Good Housekeeping,* February 1952, 52–53.
"Bores of 1962." *Nation,* 22 December 1962, 437.
"The Boy Who Was Different." *Saturday Evening Post,* November 1980, 16.
"Cat, Mouse, Man, Woman." *Contact* 1 (February 1958): 8.
"Doctors Didn't Understand." *Saturday Evening Post,* 16 August 1958, 26–27.
"The Dusty, Smeared, Musty, Moldy, Tattered Life of P. T. Barnum." *Saturday Evening Post,* 13 June 1964, 70–71.
"The End of the War and Robert Burns." *Ararat* 3 (Summer 1962): 2–5.
"Escape by Steerage." *Frontier and Midland,* May 1930, 313–21.
"Event of Enormous Beauty." *Saturday Evening Post,* 8 August 1964, 84–85.
"Father and Son." *Cosmopolitan,* August 1955, 50–55.
"A Few Excerpts from the Diary of a Corporal of the Salvation Army." In *The State of the Nation: 11 Interpretations.* Cincinnati, Ohio: Little Man Press, 1940.
"For Love of Daisy." *Saturday Evening Post,* 31 May 1958, 22–23.
"The Funny Business of Marriage." *Saturday Evening Post,* 5 October 1963, 44–45.
"Help, the Newsboy Hollered." *McCall's,* May 1967, 88–89.
"How I Met Joe Gould." *Don Freeman's Newsstand,* April 1941, 25, 27.
"In the Land of the Midnight Sun." *Saturday Evening Post,* 22 September 1962, 38.
"The Inventor and the Actress." *Atlantic Monthly,* October 1955, 55–58.
"Isn't Today the Day." *Harper's,* March 1973, 74–77.
"It's Me, O Lord." *Saturday Evening Post,* 18 April 1964, 75–76.
"Jack Levitz." *Newsstand,* Winter 1941, 13, 15, 17.
"Karl and Josef." *Scholastic Magazine,* 15 October 1938, 17–18.

"Me." *Saturday Evening Post*, 9 March 1963, 54–59.

"Meditations on the Letter Z." *Harper's*, November 1977, 118–19.

"The Miraculous Phonograph Record." *Saturday Evening Post*, 19 October 1963, 84–85.

"My Father's Sleeplessness." In *Keghouni: Armenian Illustrated Review*. Venice: San Lazzaro, 1950.

"My Lousy Adventures with Money." *Atlantic Monthly*, April 1962, 119–22.

"Mystery." *Twice a Year* 3/4 (Fall/Winter 1939–Spring/Summer 1940): 264–66.

"The Oldest Story." *Saturday Evening Post*, 11 May 1963, 54–60.

"An Ornery Kind of Kid." *Saturday Evening Post*, 15 October 1949, 26–27.

"Our Greatest Man." *Saturday Evening Post*, 12 March 1966, 80–81.

"Paris Is the Place for You." *Saturday Evening Post*, 30 September 1961, 72–73.

"Pointy Shoes." *Saturday Evening Post*, 22 May 1965, 44–46.

"The Poor World Turning." *Seven* 2 (August 1938): 24–27.

"A Remembrance of Walking." *Twice a Year* 3/4 (Fall/Winter 1939–Spring/Summer 1940): 266–70.

"Saroyan's Paris." *Story*, February 1962, 73–79.

"Shout Armenia Wherever You Go." *Saturday Evening Post*, 21 November 1964, 74.

"A Small Boy's Adventure." *Parent's Magazine*, June 1951, 38–39.

"The Smartest Nationality." *Harper's*, 8 June 1975, 8–9.

"The Story of the Man Who Fell out of a Tree." *Nation*, 21 February 1972, 247–48.

"The Sweetheart of Company D." In *The Best from "Yank," the Army Weekly*, Edited by the editors of *Yank*, 136–37. New York: E. P. Dutton, 1945.

"Take Her to Vegas." *Saturday Evening Post*, 23 September 1961, 48–49.

"Thank You Very Much for Everything and Don't Worry." *McCall's*, January 1961, 90–91.

"There's One in Every School." *Ladies' Home Journal*, February 1972, 98–99.

"Thoughts while Goldbricking." In *The Best from "Yank," the Army Weekly*, Edited by the editors of *Yank*, 281–82. New York: Royal Books, 1953.

"Three Tales." *Saturday Evening Post*, 7 October 1967, 68–70.

"The Time Before." *Booster* 4 (December 1937–January 1938): 6–7.

"To Be Courteous to Women." In *The Bedside Playboy*, Edited by Hugh M. Hefner, 327–32. Chicago: Playboy Press, 1963.

"Two Stories of World's Gone By." *Twice a Year* 3/4 (Fall/Winter 1939): 264–70.

"War and Sport Notes." *Twice a Year* 5/6 (Spring/Summer 1940): 194–98.

"Wedding Photography." *Saturday Evening Post*, March 1976, 32–34.

"What's Going on around Here?" *Seventeen*, November 1962, 152.

"Wild Boy." *Saturday Evening Post*, 25 January 1964, 32.

"The World Is Too Much Water." *Highlights from "Yank," the Army Weekly,* Edited by the editors of *Yank,* 135–37. New York: Royal Books, 1953.

Memoirs

After Thirty Years. New York: Harcourt, Brace & World, 1964. A reprint of *The Daring Young Man on the Flying Trapeze and Other Stories,* together with a series of essays about writing it.
The Bicycle Rider in Beverly Hills. New York: Scribner, 1952.
Births. Berkeley, Calif.: Creative Arts Book, 1979.
Chance Meetings. New York: W.W. Norton, 1978.
Days of Life and Death and Escape to the Moon. New York: Dial, 1970.
Here Comes There Goes You Know Who. New York: Simon & Schuster, 1961.
My Kind of Crazy and Wonderful People. New York: Harcourt, Brace & World, 1966.
Not Dying. New York: Harcourt, Brace & World, 1963.
Obituaries. Berkeley, Calif.: Creative Arts Book, 1979.
Places Where I've Done Time. New York: Praeger Publishers, 1972.
Short Drive, Sweet Chariot. New York: Phaedra, 1967.
Sons Come and Go, Mothers Hang in Forever. New York: McGraw-Hill, 1976.
The Twin Adventures. New York: Harcourt, Brace, 1950. Reprints *The Adventures of Wesley Jackson* with Saroyan's journal during the writing of the novel.

Novels

The Adventures of Wesley Jackson. New York: Harcourt, Brace, 1944.
Boys and Girls Together. New York: Harcourt, Brace & World, 1963.
The Laughing Matter. Garden City, N.Y.: Doubleday, 1953.
Mama I Love You. Boston: Little, Brown/Atlantic Monthly Press, 1956.
One Day in the Afternoon of the World. New York: Harcourt, Brace & World, 1964.
Papa You're Crazy. Boston: Little, Brown/Atlantic Monthly Press, 1957.
Rock Wagram. Garden City, N.Y.: Doubleday, 1952.
Tracy's Tiger. Garden City, N.Y.: Doubleday, 1951.

Plays

An Armenian Trilogy. Fresno: California State University Press, 1986.
The Cave Dwellers. New York: Putnam's, 1958.
A Decent Birth, a Happy Funeral. New York: Samuel French, 1958.
The Dogs, or the Paris Comedy and Two Other Plays. New York: Phaedra, 1969.
Don't Go Away Mad and Two Other Plays. New York: Harcourt, Brace, 1949.
Get Away Old Man. New York: Harcourt, Brace, 1944.

Selected Bibliography

Hello Out There. New York: Samuel French, 1976.
Jim Dandy. Cincinnati, Ohio: Little Man Press, 1941.
My Heart's in the Highlands. New York: Harcourt, Brace, 1939.
Once around the Block. New York: Samuel French, 1959.
The People with Light Coming out of Them. New York: Free Company, 1941.
The Ping-Pong Game. New York: Samuel French, 1940.
Razzle-Dazzle. New York: Harcourt, Brace, 1942.
Sam, the Highest Jumper of Them All, or the London Comedy. London: Faber & Faber, 1961.
The Slaughter of the Innocents. New York: Samuel French, 1958.
The Time of Your Life. New York: Harcourt, Brace, 1939.
Three Plays: The Beautiful People, Sweeney in the Trees, Across the Board on Tomorrow Morning. New York: Harcourt, Brace, 1941.
Three Plays: My Heart's in the Highlands, The Time of Your Life, Love's Old Sweet Song. New York: Harcourt, Brace, 1940.
Two Short Plays of 1974. Northridge, Calif.: Santa Susana Press, 1979.

Miscellaneous

Harlem as Seen by Hirschfeld. New York: Hyperion Press, 1941.
Hilltop Russians in San Francisco. San Francisco: James Dellein, 1941.
I Used to Believe I Had Forever Now I'm Not So Sure. New York: Cowles, 1968. Although conventionally listed under short stories, this book belongs there only under the broadest definition of "story." In fact, it consists essentially of miscellaneous works—reviews, essays, and so forth—that Saroyan had not yet collected in book form.
Look at Us: Us? US? With photographs by Arthur Rothstein. New York: Cowles, 1967.
Morris Hirschfield. New York: Rizzoli International, 1976.
Words and Paragraphs. Chicago: Follett, 1970.

Children's books

Horsey Gorsey and the Frog. Chippewa Falls, Wis.: Hale, 1965.
Me. New York: Crowell-Collier, 1963.
The Tooth and My Father. Garden City, N.Y.: Doubleday, 1974.

Secondary Works

Books and Special Issues of Magazines
Calonne, David Stephen. *William Saroyan: My Real Work Is Being.* Chapel Hill: University of North Carolina Press, 1983.

Selected Bibliography

Floan, Howard R. *William Saroyan*. New York: Twayne Publishers, 1966.
Foard, Elizabeth C. *William Saroyan: A Reference Guide*. Boston: G. K. Hall, 1989.
Foster, Edward Halsey. *William Saroyan*. Boise, Idaho: Western Writers Seris, 1984.
Hamalian, Leo, ed. "A Special Issue on William Saroyan." *Ararat* 25 (Spring 1984). Most of the critical and biographical material in this issue is included in Hamalian's *William Saroyan: The Man and the Writer Remembered*.
————. *William Saroyan: The Man and the Writer Remembered*. Rutherford, N.J.: Fairleigh Dickinson University Press, 1987. Includes essays, memoirs, and appreciations by Leo Hamalian, Brian Darwent, Edward Halsey Foster, S. A. Robbins, Edward Loomis, Peter Sourian, Alfred Kazin, Harry Keyishian, Daniel Leary, Dickran Kouymjian, R. C. McIntyre, Jack Warner, James Tashjian, Brenda Najimian-Magarity, Pennfield Jensen, Edward Hagopian, Aram Saroyan, Gillisann Haroian, Herbert Gold, David Kherdian, Pete Hamill, Arthur Sainer, Joel Oppenheimer, Jack Trevor Story, Jules Archer, James Laughlin, William Childress, Clark Blaise, and Aram Kevorkian. Also included are an interview with Saroyan, by Garid Basmadjian, and a selected bibliography of Saroyan's books, by Linda Hamalian.
Lee, Lawrence, and Barry Gifford. *Saroyan: A Biography*. New York: Harper & Row, 1984.
Saroyan, Aram. *Last Rites: The Death of William Saroyan*. New York: William Morrow, 1982.
————. *William Saroyan*. New York: Harcourt Brace Jovanovich, 1983.
Tashjian, James H., ed. "Saroyan Memorial Issue." *Armenian Review* 36, no. 3 (September 1981).

Articles and Parts of Books

Angoff, Charles. "William Saroyan: Some Footnotes." In *The Tone of the Twenties and Other Essays*, 205–08. New York: Barnes & Noble, 1966.
Arlen, Michael. *Passage to Ararat*. New York: Farrar, Straus & Giroux, 1975, 41–54.
Balakian, Nona. "The World of William Saroyan." In *Critical Encounters: Literary Views and Reviews, 1953–1977*, 162–78. Indianapolis: Bobbs-Merrill, 1978.
Bedrosian, Margaret. "William Saroyan and the Family Matter." *MELUS* 9, no. 4 (Winter, 1982): 13–24.
Bowen, Elizabeth. "In Spite of the Words." *New Republic*, 9 March 1953, 18–19.
Burgum, Edwin B. "The Lonesome Young Man on the Flying Trapeze." *Virginia Quarterly Review* 20 (Summer 1944): 392–403.
Caen, Herb. Introduction to William Saroyan, *The Man with the Heart in the*

Highlands and Other Early Stories. New York: New Directions, 1989. vii–x.

Carpenter, Frederic I. "The Time of Saroyan's Life." *Pacific Spectator* 1 (Winter 1947): 88–96.

Darwent, Brian. "William Saroyan: A Biographical Sketch." In *The New Saroyan Reader: A Connoisseur's Anthology of the Writings of William Saroyan,* ix–xix. Berkeley, Calif.: Creative Arts Books, 1984.

Fisher, William J. "What Ever Happened to Saroyan?" *College English* 16 (March 1955): 336–40.

Floan, Howard R. "Saroyan and Cervantes' Knight." *Thought* 33 (Spring 1958): 81–92.

Gold, Herbert. "A Twenty-Year Talk with Saroyan." *New York Times Book Review,* 20 May 1979, 7, 49–50. Reprinted in *A Walk on the West Side: California on the Brink.* New York: Arbor House, 1981.

Haslam, Gerald W. "William Saroyan." In *A Literary History of the American West,* 472–81. Fort Worth: Texas Christian University Press, 1987.

Hatcher, Harlan. "William Saroyan." *English Journal* 28 (March 1939): 167–77.

Keyishian, Harry. "Michael Arlen and William Saroyan: Armenian Ethnicity and the Writer." In *The Old Century and the New,* edited by Bruno Rosa, 192–206. Rutherford, N.J.: Fairleigh Dickinson University Press, 1979.

Kouymjian, Dickram. Introduction to William Saroyan, *An Armenian Trilogy.* Fresno: California State University Press, 1986.

Krickel, Edward. "Cozzens and Saroyan: A Look at Two Reputations." *Georgia Review* 24 (Fall 1970): 281–96.

Nathan, George Jean. "Saroyan: Whirling Dervish of Fresno." *American Mercury* 51 (November 1940): 303–8.

Petite, Joseph. "Saroyan's 'Laughter.'" *Explicator* 43, no.3 (Spring 1985): 41–42.

Rahv, Philip. "Narcissus" (review of *The Daring Young Man*). *Partisan Review* 2, no. 6 (June 1935): 84–85.

———. "William Saroyan: A Minority Report." *American Mercury* 57 (September 1943): 371–77.

Remenyi, Joseph. "William Saroyan: A Portrait." *College English* 6 (November 1944): 92–100.

Schorer, Mark. "Technique as Discovery." In *The World We Imagine,* 3–23. New York: Farrar, Straus & Giroux, 1968.

Schulberg, Budd. "Saroyan: Ease and Unease on the Flying Trapeze." *Esquire,* October 1960, 85–91. Reprinted in *The Four Seasons of Success,* 55–87. Garden City, N.Y.: Doubleday, 1972.

Shear, Walter. "Saroyan's Study of Ethnicity." *MELUS* 13 (Spring/Summer 1986): 45–55.

Tashjian, James H. "A Preface (and Other Things)." In William Saroyan, *My Name Is Saroyan,* 13–36. New York: Harcourt Brace Jovanovich, 1983.

Wilson, Edmund. "The Boys in the Back Room." In *Classics and Commercials.* New York: Farrar, Straus, 1950.

Index

The Author

Edward Halsey Foster is a professor of English and American literature at the Stevens Institute of Technology. His books include *Catharine Maria Sedgwick* (1974), *The Civilized Wilderness* (1975), *Josiah Gregg and Lewis H. Garrard* (1977), *Susan and Anna Warner* (1978), *Richard Brautigan* (1983), *William Saroyan* (1984), and *Jack Spicer* (1991). He is at present completing a study of the San Francisco Poetry Renaissance and a study of the beat writers. The recipient of various grants and awards from the National Endowment for the Humanities, Columbia University, the New Jersey State Council on the Arts, and the Fulbright Commission, he has also published numerous articles and reviews and has lectured extensively both in the United States and abroad. He edits *Talisman: A Journal of Contemporary Poetry and Poetics*. Married and the father of two children, he divides his time between New York City and a farm in the Berkshires.

The Editor

Gordon Weaver earned his Ph.D. in English and creative writing at the University of Denver, and is currently professor of English at Oklahoma State University. He is the author of several novels, including *Count a Lonely Cadence, Give Him a Stone, Circling Byzantium,* and most recently *The Eight Corners of the World.* His short stories are collected in *The Entombed Man of Thule, Such Waltzing Was Not Easy, Getting Serious, Morality Play,* and *A World Quite Round.* Recognition of his fiction includes the St. Lawrence Award for Fiction (1973), two National Endowment for the Arts fellowships (1974 and 1989), and the O. Henry First Prize (1979). He edited *The American Short Story, 1945–1980: A Critical History* and is currently editor of the *Cimarron Review.* Married and the father of three daughters, he lives in Stillwater, Oklahoma.